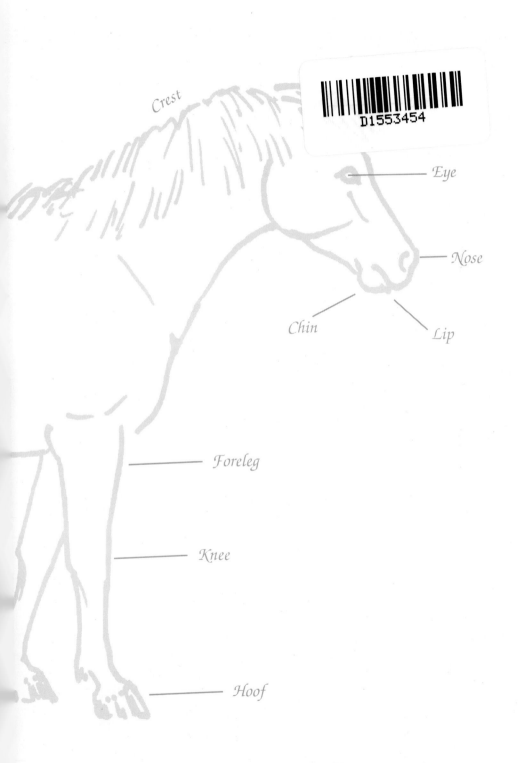

Crest

Eye

Nose

Chin

Lip

Foreleg

Knee

Hoof

A PRACTICAL FIELD GUIDE TO
HORSE BEHAVIOR

The Equid Ethogram

A PRACTICAL FIELD GUIDE TO
HORSE BEHAVIOR

The Equid Ethogram

Sue McDonnell, Ph.D.

A Division of The Blood-Horse, Inc.
PUBLISHERS SINCE 1916

Library of Congress Control Number: 2002110116

ISBN 1-58150-090-4

Printed in Hong Kong
First Edition: January 2003

Distributed to the trade by
National Book Network
4720-A Boston Way, Lanham, MD 20706
1.800.462.6420

ECLIPSE
PRESS

A Division of The Blood-Horse, Inc.
PUBLISHERS SINCE 1916

MAINTENANCE BEHAVIOR

GENERAL SOCIAL COMMUNICATION

INTERMALE INTERACTION

PLAY

DOMESTICALLY SHAPED AND ABERRANT BEHAVIOR

PREFACE

More than fifteen years ago, out of specific research project needs, our lab at the University of Pennsylvania's New Bolton Center started collecting descriptive definitions, line drawings, and photos of horse behaviors as a method of objectively defining these behaviors. It was quite amazing to us and to other equine behavior colleagues that with all the interest in horses over the centuries, a comprehensive catalog of equine behavior had not been published in the scientific literature. Year after year we grumbled about this scientific travesty at the outset of projects, and at the end of projects we tossed our lists and working definitions as well as photos and drawings into a box, labeled *Equid Ethogram Stuff*, kept under the conference room stairwell. At each annual student research day we proudly listed among the lab's accomplishments the contributions toward the long-term goal of compiling a complete equid ethogram. In other words, we put more stuff in the box. Soon it seemed like enough stuff to ask ourselves, Why not put it all together? Make a list of behaviors, for each pick the best common name, write a descriptive definition, list other names by which each has been identified in the literature, add pertinent comments, list the species of equids in which it has been defined, select representative photos, put all the entries into meaningful categories, and there you have it — a complete ethogram of the horse.

It soon became apparent that developing an ethogram for the narrowly focused specific studies or experiments we do each year would be a lot simpler than a comprehensive ethogram of everything that horses do. Just how should it be organized, in how much detail? Go with an anatomical or with a functional approach when defining a particular aspect of behavior? For example, do we call the precopulatory sequence of "sniffing the head, body, perineum" just that or call it "teasing" or "courtship"? Verb or noun names ("eat" or "eating"); do you need consistency — or which is better? We soon started to wonder how many other equid ethograms might have been started over the years and then put back in their boxes amidst similar thoughtful indecision.

So we sought advice from colleagues, sending drafts around the world of equine behavior for review. They diligently marked them up, and soon we felt like the master's degree student whose thesis draft comes back from the committee members with completely contradictory advice in all directions. With that, we decided to get started with the ethogram. Just take the first step — publish our best shot at it, lay it on the table for comment and discussion, and then start another box under the stairwell, this time *Ethogram Additions/Corrections/Suggestions*. Hopefully, we'll be inundated with advice, and there will be chances for improved editions.

What is an ethogram?

An ethogram is one of the basic organizational tools used to study behavior. Ethogram comes from the European name for the study of natural behavior, or *ethology*. In classic ethology, the first step in understanding a species' behavior and how it is influenced is a precise listing and description of each behavior observed. So an ethogram for any species is a formal catalog of the various behavior sequences and the individual behavioral elements comprising those sequences. Ethograms were popularized in the middle of the last century with the work of Conrad Lorenz, Niko Timbergen, and Karl von Frisch, who in 1973 won the Nobel Prize in medicine for their work in animal behavior.

Ethograms have been constructed in many forms and levels of completeness and detail, depending upon their purpose. For example, an ethogram can comprehensively classify most behaviors of a species. But a comprehensive ethogram is rare because of the magnitude of the undertaking and the ever more specialized focus of researchers. An ethogram can be even more focused on a specific sequence, such as a mare and foal interacting (maternal-neonatal interaction) or a mare helping her foal to nurse (maternal facilitation of suckling). Ethograms can take many forms, from structured flow charts and diagrams of stimulus-response sequences or encyclopedic catalogs to simple lists of behaviors. The format, details, and organization of any ethogram depend upon the purpose.

As far as we know, a comprehensive ethogram has not been published for any of the equids. Most of the original scientific descriptions of equid behavior under natural conditions that appear in English were part of graduate studies during the 1970s. For example, James Feist's 1971 master's thesis from the University of Michigan described a good portion of the behavioral repertoire of wild horses studied in the Pryor Mountain Wild Horse Range. Similarly, Patricia Moehlman's 1974 doctoral dissertation from the University of Wisconsin described a considerable portion of the behavior of feral asses studied in the Death Valley National Monument. For Przewalski horses, Lee Boyd and Katherine Houpt (1994) developed a detailed outline of the behavioral repertoire of those species under captive conditions. More commonly, equid ethograms have been limited to a particular class of behavior under study at the time, such as aggressive behavior, maternal behavior, or foraging behavior.

How was this ethogram compiled and formatted?

This ethogram was compiled with two general purposes. The first is to facilitate communication among people interested in horse behavior by organizing existing information and standardizing nomenclature in English. Whether one is a senior scientist, a graduate student starting a thesis project, a middle-schooler studying animal behavior, or a horse enthusiast, it's useful to have an organized, accurate guide to the literature. The second purpose of this ethogram is to serve as a field guide for anyone interested in observing horse behavior, whether formally as a trained biologist or informally as a horse owner or enthusiast.

This ethogram is organized as a semi-comprehensive catalog of specific behaviors. The focal species is the horse, as it appeals to a broader audience than other equids. While example references to Przewalski horse, donkey, and zebra species are provided, one obvious addition might have been further comparative details, including the interesting variations and differences in behavior among the equid species. However, occasional comments on their interesting differences of behavior are included.

Each section represents a general category of behavior. The categories chosen are commonly used for mammals. Each section includes a brief introduction, followed by behavior entries for the most common specific behaviors observed in horses or in the scientific literature. Each behavior entry includes a name, line drawing, description, and additional information of interest to people studying horse behavior, such as other species in which the behavior has been described. This format was selected for simplicity and for consolidation of information.

The goal is to provide a user-friendly, practical field guide for equine behavior researchers and hobbyists, veterinarians, and students of all ages while also offering enough references to get serious students started on further scientific study.

Compiling and organizing this ethogram have been fun. All those who have contributed trust that it will be a useful tool for your observation and understanding of horse behavior.

Sue McDonnell
New Bolton Center
Kennett Square, Pennsylvania

ACKNOWLEDGMENTS

The main sources of information for this ethogram were the scientific-behavior literature available in English; our laboratory field notes, photographs, and video recordings; and fifteen years of recollections from original observations of equids (both casual and formal). The veterinary behavior research trainees in our laboratory also contributed. These trainees are mostly veterinary students, with some pre-veterinary, biology, animal science, and animal behavior undergraduates. These students took many of the photographs of our semi-feral pony herd that illustrate this ethogram.

Dr. Jean Schultz Haviland, now a mixed-practice veterinarian, worked for two summers during veterinary school studying intermale interactions, organizing the catalog, sketching line depictions, and obtaining representative photographs. Jean was co-author of our resulting original scientific publication (McDonnell and Haviland 1994). Dr. Michael Fugaro, now an equine practitioner, assisted with Jean's fieldwork while he was a pre-veterinary student in animal science at the University of Delaware. Lee Ann Toolan, now an equine practitioner in Canada, also assisted Jean. At the time, Lee Ann was a research trainee from the Western College of Veterinary Medicine at the University of Saskatoon. Jen Plebani, now a doctoral candidate in psychology at the University of Vermont, contributed to the intermale interaction section with work done here while she was earning her master's degree in animal behavior in the psychology department at West Chester University.

Dr. Samantha Murray, now a small-animal surgery resident at the University of Pennsylvania School of Veterinary Medicine, also assisted with sections on intermale interaction, sexual behavior, play and development, parturition, and parenting behavior. This was done over summer and holiday vacations during high school and while an undergraduate studying animal science at the University of Delaware.

Dr. Elizabeth Hochsprung Ewaskiewicz, now an equine practitioner in central Pennsylvania, contributed during the summers of 1996 and 1997 while in veterinary school here at Penn to sections on parturition, parenting, and particularly the interaction of stallions with juveniles. Dr. Melissa Lutz, now a mixed-practice veterinarian, similarly spent the summer of 1997. Her focus was on early foal development behavior.

Amy Poulin, now nearly finished with veterinary school at Penn, spent her summer between college and veterinary school drafting the original scientific paper on which the section on play is based (McDonnell and Poulin 2002).

Elkanah Grogan, who has been managing our semi-feral herd and working on a variety of equine behavior research projects while studying animal science at the University of Delaware, assisted with literature reviews and contributed the majority of the photographs selected for publication.

In addition, section drafts were circulated to equine-behavior researchers worldwide. They included Leo Baskin, Judith Blackshaw, Lee Boyd, Frank Bristol, Sharon Cregier, Jim Crump, Nancy Diehl, Patrick Duncan, Daniel Estep, Andrew Fraser, Katherine Houpt, Carys Hughes, M. Jaworowska, Ronald Keiper, Jocelyn Kish, B Penzhorn, Daniel Mills, Malgorzata Pozor, A. Rasa, H. Rifa, Sarah Ralston, Daniel Rubenstein, M. Schilder, Machteld van Dierendonck, Victoria Voith, Natalie Waran, Stephan Wierzbowski, and David Wood-Gush. Several important additions and clarifications from these colleagues were incorporated.

Most of the original observations supporting this ethogram were conducted within the context of a semi-feral herd of

Shetland-type ponies that resides at New Bolton Center of the University of Pennsylvania School of Veterinary Medicine. This herd was started by assembling at pasture a group of mature pony mares and stallions obtained from local auctions and farms. They have been maintained there since 1994 with minimal intervention. They serve primarily as a living laboratory readily available year-round for study of physiology and behavior. They also serve as an educational resource for veterinary and animal behavior students and, on a limited basis, the seriously interested horse-owning public. The herd includes multiple harem groups with foals, yearlings, and some young adult offspring, as well as bachelor and young juvenile groups. The herd quickly grew to fill the available acreage, and so has been maintained at between 50 and 75 animals. As necessary, entire family groups are separated from the main herd and are then gently introduced to the domestic environment before eventually ending up as ordinary domestic ponies.

Erlene Michener has tirelessly prepared the line drawings for this book as well as for our scientific papers. Erlene is an extraordinary horsewoman, nature conservancy educator, medical illustrator, and artist with a special appreciation for the details of animal behavior.

Jackie Duke of Eclipse Press and The Blood-Horse Publishing group took on this challenging book project. In the spirit of bringing scientifically sound information to the wider equine audience, they worked diligently with us to produce a book of high academic quality that is user-friendly and affordable to students and horse enthusiasts.

This book is dedicated to Bob Kenney and Shirley Fox

INTRODUCTION
General social organization of equids

All of the equid species remaining today can be divided into two general types of social organization: territorial breeders or harem breeders. The horses, their primitive living ancestor the Przewalski horses (*Equus przewalskii*), and the common zebras (*Equus burchelli, Equus quagga,* and *Equus zebra*) are harem breeders, while Grevy's zebra (*Equus grevyi*) and asses (*Equus africanus, Equus hemionus, Equus asinus*) are territorial breeders.

Harem Breeders

The harem type equids tend to live in large herds comprising several smaller bands. The basic breeding family groups are known as harem bands. Each harem band consists of one mature breeding male known as the harem stallion, a few mature breeding females (mares), and their young offspring. The harem stallion stays with his mares and their young offspring all year. The stallion herds and protects the females and young from co-mingling with other bands. The harem stallion also directs the movement of the family whenever it is threatened or near other bands. The harem stallion performs marking sequences in which he investigates and covers his mares' feces and urine with his own. Although the harem stallions often appear to human intruders as completely "in charge" of their harem's activities, leadership is usually limited to defense from intruders. The actual leader of a harem group in everyday maintenance activities is usually a mature mare. So, for example, treks to water, movement to a new grazing area, or shifts within the day from grazing to resting are typically led by a mare.

Dr. Hans Klingel first summarized the classifications of equid social organization in 1975, based on his studies of equids around the world. A complete list of Klingel's scientific publications, as well as his collection of scientific references as of June 2002 can be found at http://www2.vet.upenn.edu/labs/equinebehavior/hvnwkshp/hv02/klingref.htm. His own original papers make for very interesting reading. The serious student of horse behavior or comparative equid behavior will likely find his early papers helpful in understanding the specific behaviors of horses and other equids.

The mares and their young appear more or less socially bonded independently of the stallion's efforts to keep them together.

A relatively rare variation of the single-stallion harem is the two-stallion harem. The second stallion is an unrelated mature male that assists the main breeding stallion. The assistant harem stallion is not allowed access to the mature family mares, but he may on rare occasion breed a young mare that is still with the natal band. The assistant's main role appears to be defense and help with keeping a large harem together.

In the harem social organization, the young stay with their natal band for one to three or more years. The first year is characterized by a large amount of play. This play takes the form of athletic locomotor play, interactive play with the environment, and social play mostly among the young. The young typically leave their natal band in one of two ways. Their sire drives some, usually maturing males, off. This can happen in an explosive confrontation or gradually over a period of months. But most appear to leave gradually on their own. Yearlings and two-year-olds tend to form affiliations with young from other harem bands. These gangs of young males and females may come and go from their natal band for as long as a year or more before leaving permanently.

In addition to the harem bands, a herd of horses includes bands of males that do not have mares. The stallions are called bachelors. They tend to stay together as close to the harem bands as the harem stallions will allow. The young females mature at about one year of age and may have their first offspring as early as two or three years of age. Young males also mature at about one to two years of age. Close affiliations often exist within bands. Mares or bachelors stallions often have preferred neighbors within their band. Bachelors often form two- and three-partner alliances to cooperate in controlling limited resources.

Territorial Breeders

In contrast to the harem social organization based on the breeding stallions guarding a stable harem of mares and their young, in territorial-type breeding equids the breeding males guard a territory. These territorial males gain breeding access to females that pass through or linger in the territory. The females travel alone with their young offspring or in loose and/or temporary pairs.

Comments on Dominance, Submission, and Hierarchies in Equids

One of the most useful topics of horse behavior at any level of study is probably *social order*, the dominance and submission within and between bands and herds of horses. The horse is an excellent example of what is known as a *social* species. Horses clearly live together and, where possible, tend to live in large herds. As such, a great deal of their behavior concerns communication among herd mates and the establishment and maintenance of a social hierarchy that enables peaceful, ongoing interaction. In addition to dominance relationships within bands of horses, a dominance order appears among the bands within a herd. This hierarchy allows orderly access to limited resources, such as the best foraging spots, as well as daily access to water, shade, and shelter. With a large, established herd, certain bands clearly appear dominant.

When you study a species under natural conditions, the beauty of social order is more apparent. It becomes obvious how domestic conditions typically interfere with horses and other managed species establishing social order. It becomes easy to understand the miscommunications and social disturbances that represent a large portion of the herd behavior problems and injuries of horses kept under modern management. For example, in undisturbed populations of horses with plenty of space, overt, serious aggression is rare. That's because the order has long before been worked out and perhaps even passed from one generation to the next within a herd. So simple head gestures and calm movement of the dominant groups and individuals appear to displace effectively submissive groups to achieve the social goals and access to resources. The most aggressive behavior occurs between closely matched pairs, often among young males straying from the natal band and "testing" their cohorts in newly forming bachelor bands.

This understanding of horse social order has many everyday practical implications. For example, you will hear folks talk about an alpha mare or an alpha stallion, implying dominance and leadership of an entire group. The label of alpha animal within a group of domestic horses is usually based on the individual's ability to control a limited resource, say a feed bunk or a row of grain buckets along a fence. We all know horses that can control such a focused resource, or create havoc trying. But this is a fairly unnatural condition created by our husbandry practice. Under natural conditions, it is rare to see overt aggression or a single individual controlling a limited resource. Surely under natural conditions, horses rarely have the equivalent of an alpha individual within a band or an alpha band within a herd. Rather, there is usually a more complex, less linear order, with division of leadership and defense roles played by a number of individuals and sometimes with alliances that swing into action depending upon the situation. So, for example, in times of threat to a harem, the harem stallion and/or assistant harem stallion typically approaches and fends off the intruder. While in times of limited resources, a mature mare or two may control initial access to the resource. And in terms of leading the group's activities, it may be yet another individual, usually a mature mare, that seems to lead the way in changing activities or direction of the group, say moving to water or shade. Similarly, dominance and leadership are not simple linear relationships of individuals. And animal *A* as an individual may be dominant over animal *B*, which is dominant over animal *C*, which is dominant over animal *A*. This is known as a *triangular* relationship. Similarly, one animal may alone be submissive to another, but with a companion, may be dominant to the same animal alone or with its companion.

The concept of dominance is commonly invoked in discussion of human-horse interaction. For example, popular horse trainers often claim that the successful human handler must take the role of a dominant horse to interact effectively with a horse. A great deal of instruction is given on body postures and gazes to communicate dominance over a horse. The horse must submit to a dominant human. Current academic horse behavior discussion would argue that in the real world of horse behavior, submission in an open plains species such as the horse means withdrawal or escape. They would further argue that most horse trainers do not really want their horse retreating with head lowered and tail tucked. While it is difficult to meaningfully compare the human-horse working relationship with that of any natural relationship, what the trainer is typically striving for is a relationship of leadership and trust, similar to that of a mature mare leading the group to water or rest or an alliance similar to that of two bachelors playing together. On the surface this may seem like the age-old argument of the academic versus the practical, but these contrasting views carry important philosophical and practical implications for the welfare of human and horse.

SECTION I

MAINTENANCE BEHAVIOR

A common classification for descriptive animal behavior is to include all the ongoing daily activities that serve to keep an animal alive and well in one category called maintenance behavior. So that would include behavior-serving nutrition and hydration, both input and output; basic movement; rest; and shelter. Authors vary in the sub-organization. The specific maintenance behaviors cataloged here are organized as ingestive behavior (both feeding and drinking), elimination, locomotion, rest, and then shelter and comfort-seeking behavior.

Excellent studies of time budgets on equids under various wild and feral conditions can provide details of daily activities of equids (Pellegrini 1971, Boy et al. 1979, Keiper and Keenan 1980, Mayes and Duncan 1986, Boyd et al. 1988, Rudman and Keiper 1991, Crowell-Davis 1994).

INGESTION

In natural environments, horses prefer grasses but will also forage and derive nutrition from bark, tree and shrub buds and leaves, small woody stems, aquatic plants, fruits, roots, and seeds (such as acorns).

Daily foraging time and patterns vary widely with the availability and nutritional value of plant materials. Except in extremely lush conditions, horses when on natural forage generally spend about 60% to 80% of their time feeding. In general, populations adopt daily and seasonal patterns of intermittent foraging and resting more or less around the clock. Peak foraging and resting patterns often coincide with the seasonal daily weather and insect conditions. For example, in summer a herd may forage during the cooler parts of the day and rest during the hottest parts of the day and may stand in water when the biting insects are out. Only severe storms with high winds or heavy downpours or thunder interfere significantly with daily grazing schedules.

Foals usually begin grazing at one to two weeks of age. Initially the behavior seems like play or "picking" rather than grazing for nutrition.

Horses ingest water in the form of moisture in and on forage. They drink from streams, pools, and rain puddles. They also ingest water in the form of frost, ice, and snow. The frequency of drinking varies considerably with environmental factors, such as the distance and availability of streams or pools, moisture ingested with forage, weather conditions (with more frequent drinking in warm conditions), and lactation. In areas where water is distant from prime foraging, bands typically trek together to water. At the watering site, bands within a group go to water in a specific order generally accepted as a dominance order.

Graze

Ingest grassy vegetation. With the lips and tongue, vegetation is gathered into the mouth, broken off usually in clumps by jerking the jaw while chewing, and swallowed.

Described in:

Horses — domestic and feral horses and ponies (Feist 1971, Tyler 1972, Waring 1983, Keiper 1985)

Przewalski horses — zoo-managed Przewalski horses (Boyd and Houpt 1994)

Donkeys — feral asses *Equus africanus* (Moehlman 1974, 1998)

Zebra — Grevy's zebra *Equus grevyi* (Gardner 1983), Cape Mountain zebra *Equus zebra zebra* (Penzhorn 1984)

Close-up of yearling *grazing*

Stallion selectively *grazing* seed heads of mature grasses

Graze Recumbent

Graze or browse while in sternal recumbency.

Comments*:* This is seen more commonly in foals, and sometimes in disabled or uncomfortable adults that appear reluctant to stand, but is sometimes seen in normal healthy adults as well.

Described in*:*

Horses — domestic horses and ponies (S McDonnell unpublished observations)

Donkeys — feral asses *Equus africanus* (Moehlman 1974, 1998)

Paw (Dig) While Foraging and Drinking

Drag a foreleg along the substrate while grazing, browsing, or seeking water, effectively removing snow or matted overgrowth covering preferred vegetation beneath, unearthing roots, or breaking ice for water.

Described in:

Horses — domestic and feral horses and ponies (Feist 1971, Tyler 1972, Waring 1983, Keiper 1985)

Przewalski horses — zoo-managed Przewalski horses (Klimov 1988)

Donkeys — feral asses *Equus africanus* (Moehlman 1974, 1998)

Zebra — Cape Mountain zebra *Equus zebra zebra* (Penzhorn 1984)

Mature mare and son *pawing* **while** *drinking*

27

Browse

Ingest woody plants.

Described in:

Horses — domestic and feral horses and ponies (Waring 1983, Keiper 1985)

Przewalski horses — zoo-managed Przewalski horses (Boyd and Houpt 1994)

Donkeys — feral asses *Equus africanus* (Moehlman 1974, 1998); feral asses *Equus asinus* (McCort 1980); semi-feral donkeys (S McDonnell unpublished observations)

Zebra — Grevy's zebra *Equus grevyi* (Gardner 1983)

Young mare *browsing*

Coprophagy

Ingest feces, by using lips and tongue to draw feces into the mouth, chew, and swallow.

Comments: Normal developmental behavior of foals (Francis-Smith and Wood-Gush 1977).

Described in:

Horses — domestic and feral horses and ponies (Hafez et al. 1962, Tyler 1972, Feist and McCullough 1976, Waring 1983, Crowell-Davis and Houpt 1985)

Przewalski horses — zoo-managed Przewalski horses (Boyd and Houpt 1994)

Donkeys — semi-feral donkeys (J Beech unpublished observations)

Zebra — Cape Mountain zebra *Equus zebra zebra* (Penzhorn 1984)

SUE MCDONNELL

Mature stallion *eating feces*

29

Pica

Ingest soil, by using the lips and tongue to draw soil into the mouth and swallow.

Described in:

Horses — feral horses (Feist 1971, Salter and Hudson 1979)

Przewalski horses — zoo-managed Przewalski horses (Boyd and Houpt 1994)

Donkeys — semi-feral donkeys (J Beech unpublished observations)

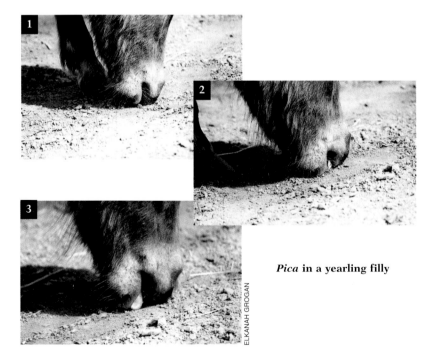

Pica in a yearling filly

ELKANAH GROGAN

Drink

Ingest water, typically by using lips at or slightly below the surface of water, and drawing water with sucking action through slightly parted lips and teeth and swallowing.

Comments: In wet areas without streams or pools, or that are in the process of drying up, horses may dig holes that fill with water or may drink from hoof impressions that have filled with water. Horses also can obtain considerable hydration by licking ice and ingesting snow.

Described in:

Horses — domestic and feral horses and ponies (Feist 1971, Tyler 1972, Waring 1983, Keiper 1985)

Przewalski horses — zoo-managed Przewalski horses (Boyd and Houpt 1994)

Donkeys — feral asses *Equus africanus* (Moehlman 1974, 1998); feral asses *Equus asinus* (McCort 1980)

Zebra — Grevy's zebra *Equus grevyi* (Gardner 1983); Cape Mountain zebra *Equus zebra zebra* (Penzhorn 1984)

Drink

Mature mare and daughter *drinking* in pond

Mares and yearling *drinking* at edge of pond

ELIMINATION

Elimination behavior in mammals includes urination, defecation, and regurgitation of ingesta. Horses do not regurgitate, and so their eliminative behavior is limited to urination and defecation. Elimination also includes marking or covering behavior associated with urine and feces.

In horses, behavior associated with elimination is *sexually dimorphic*, which means there are distinct male and female forms. Females urinate and defecate "ad lib" with fairly random placement. There is no associated attention to the excrement, such as sniffing, pawing, or covering, to their own or other conspecific (same species) feces or urine. In stallions, defecation occurs at specific fecal accumulations or "stud piles" often positioned at apparently meaningful locations along commonly traveled routes or near limited resources such as watering sites. Significant olfactory investigating and pawing may both precede and follow defecation of males. A significant portion of the urination of harem stallions occurs within the context of marking of eliminations of the harem group members. Harem stallions approach and cover the urinations and defecations of the group members.

For females and juvenile males, ongoing activities are only momentarily interrupted by urination and sometimes not at all for defecation. For stallions, elimination and the associated behaviors often significantly interrupt ongoing activity.

The amount and frequency of elimination vary with the availability of food and water, as well as with the weather and exercise conditions. So urination or defecation may be as infrequent as two or three times a day or as often as once every two or three hours.

Urination, Male

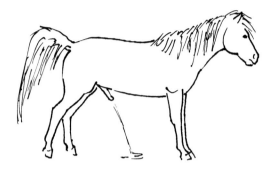

With forelegs slightly extended forward and hind legs extended backward and slightly spread, expelling of urine through the urethra. The penis is typically partially or fully relaxed from the prepuce.

Comments*:* Urination and defecation during ongoing activities typically are separate events. In windy conditions, horses may face into the wind for urination (Tyler 1972).

Described in*:*

Horses — domestic and feral horses and ponies (Feist 1971, Tyler 1972, Waring 1983, Keiper 1985)

Przewalski horses — zoo-managed Przewalski horses (Boyd and Houpt 1994)

Donkeys — feral asses *Equus africanus* (Moehlman 1974, 1998); feral asses *Equus asinus* (McCort 1980)

Zebra — Grevy's zebra *Equus grevyi* (Gardner 1983); Cape Mountain zebra *Equus zebra zebra* (Penzhorn 1984)

Days-old colt *urinating*

Urination with *Flehmen response* in a colt

Mature stallion *urinating*

Urination, Female

With the back arched, the tail raised, and the hind limbs extended backward and separated (without squatting), expelling of urine through the urethra and vulva. Final small quantities are expelled with vulvar contractions that commence after the main stream.

Comments: Ongoing grazing, walking, or resting is interrupted momentarily for urination in females. Urination and defecation during ongoing activities are typically separate events. Mares with foals have been described as posturing more profoundly as if to avoid splashing the udder (Hafez et al. 1962). In windy conditions, horses face into the wind for urination (Tyler 1972).

Described in:

Horses — domestic and feral horses and ponies (Feist 1971, Tyler 1972, Waring 1983, Keiper 1985)

Przewalski horses — zoo-managed Przewalski horses (Boyd and Houpt 1994)

Donkeys — feral asses *Equus africanus* (Moehlman 1974, 1998); feral asses *Equus asinus* (McCort 1980)

Zebra — Cape Mountain zebra *Equus zebra zebra* (Penzhorn 1984)

ELIZABETH EWASKIEWICZ

Week-old female *urinating*

SUE MCDONNELL

Yearling filly *urinating*

Defecation

With tail raised, expelling of feces through the anus. The anal sphincter contracts rhythmically and the tail may be lashed vertically at the completion of passage of feces. The mare simply postures, defecates, and walks off following defecation. The stallion sniffs and may paw at the site before and again after defecation, with Flehmen response, whether or not further *elimination marking sequence* behaviors are included.

Comments: Same basic posture for expelling feces in males and females. Urination and defecation during ongoing activities do not usually occur as related events.

Described in:

Horses — domestic and feral horses and ponies (Feist 1971, Tyler 1972, Waring 1983, Keiper 1985)

Przewalski horses — zoo-managed Przewalski horses (Boyd and Houpt 1994)

Donkeys — feral asses *Equus africanus* (Moehlman 1974, 1998); feral asses *Equus asinus* (McCort 1980)

Zebra — Grevy's zebra *Equus grevyi* (Gardner 1983); Cape Mountain zebra *Equus zebra zebra* (Penzhorn 1984)

Mature stallion *defecating*

LOCOMOTION

In the study of animal behavior, locomotion is usually defined as voluntary movement of the whole body on land, in water, or in air. As with most terrestrial mammals, locomotion for equids includes walking, running, jumping, and swimming.

Locomotion in the horse begins within the first hour of life and reaches a full complement of locomotor abilities within the first day and then continues until soon before death.

Horses can and do often travel many miles per day for grazing, water, and resting sites. They can cross water and rugged terrain at good speeds.

This discussion of locomotion begins with the standing alert posture as a reference, followed by the common gaits, group movements, jumping, and swimming.

Stand Alert

Rigid stance with the neck elevated and the head oriented toward the object or animal of focus. The ears are held stiffly upright and forward, and the nostrils may be slightly dilated. Similar to the *Alert* of intermale interaction (Section III, page 106).

Other names: *stand-stare* (Feist 1971), *stare* (Waring 1983), *standing alert* (Duncan 1985), *vigilance* (Berger 1986), *attention face* (zebra, Schilder and Boer 1987), and, if the animal turns the body to face the object of interest, *turn toward* (asses, McCort 1980).

Comments: *Alert* posture may be followed by approach, followed by either friendly or aggressive interactions, or by resumption of the previous activity.

Described in:

Horses — domestic and feral horses and ponies (Feist 1971, Tyler 1972, Waring 1983, Keiper 1985)

Przewalski horses — zoo-managed Przewalski horses (Boyd and Houpt 1994)

Donkeys — feral asses *Equus africanus* (Moehlman 1974, 1998); feral asses *Equus asinus* (McCort 1980)

Zebra — Grevy's zebra *Equus grevyi* (Gardner 1983); Cape Mountain zebra *Equus zebra zebra* (Penzhorn 1984)

Mare *alert*

ELKANAH GROGAN

Walk

Slow Walk

Alert Walk

Movement forward in the slowest (four beat) of the mammalian quadrupedal gaits.

Other names: Acquired variations include *flat-footed walk* (slowest); *running walk* (faster); *rack* (fastest) (Evans 1989).

Comments: Horses walk continuously while they graze. They typically take a few bites at each stop before moving forward two or three steps to a new "patch."

Described in:

Horses — domestic and feral horses and ponies (Waring 1983)

Przewalski horses — zoo-managed Przewalski horses (Boyd and Houpt 1994)

Donkeys — feral asses *Equus africanus* (Moehlman 1974, 1998); feral asses *Equus asinus* (McCort 1980)

Zebra — Grevy's zebra *Equus grevyi* (Gardner 1983)

Walk

Harem *walking*

ELKANAH GROGAN

Trot

Movement forward in a two-beat gait, in which diagonally paired feet touch and lift simultaneously.

Comments: Natural variations of the trot are referred to as "extended" and "collected" (Evans 1989).

Described in:

Horses — domestic and feral horses and ponies (Waring 1983)

Przewalski horses — zoo-managed Przewalski horses (Boyd and Houpt 1994)

Donkeys — feral asses *Equus africanus* (Moehlman 1974, 1998); feral asses *Equus asinus* (McCort 1980)

Zebra — Grevy's zebra *Equus grevyi* (Gardner 1983)

SUE MCDONNELL

Mare and young foal *trotting*

Trot

Young stallion *trotting* to rejoin his bachelor group

Trotting **bachelor being followed by *cantering* cohort**

Canter

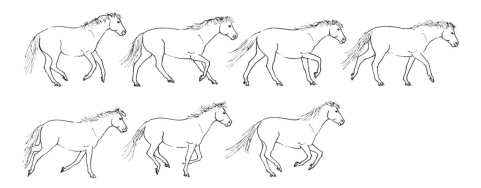

Running in a three-beat medium-speed gait.

Other names: *lope* (Evans 1989), *canter-gallop* (asses, Moehlman 1974, 1998).

Described in:

Horses — domestic and feral horses and ponies (Waring 1983)

Przewalski horses — zoo-managed Przewalski horses (Boyd and Houpt 1994)

Donkeys — feral asses *Equus africanus* (Moehlman 1974, 1998); feral asses *Equus asinus* (McCort 1980)

Yearlings *cantering*

Gallop

Running fast with a four-beat gait.

Other names: *run* (Evans 1989), *canter-gallop* (asses, Moehlman 1974, 1998).

Described in:

Horses — domestic and feral horses and ponies (Waring 1983)

Przewalski horses — zoo-managed Przewalski horses (Boyd and Houpt 1994)

Donkeys — feral asses *Equus africanus* (Moehlman 1974, 1998)

Zebra — Grevy's zebra *Equus grevyi* (Gardner 1983)

Bachelor stallion *galloping* after a companion bachelor

46

Trek

Two or more animals moving a distance together, typically following one after the other.

Described in:

Horses — domestic and feral horses and ponies (Feist 1971, Tyler 1972, Waring 1983, Keiper 1985)

Donkeys — feral asses *Equus asinus* (McCort 1980)

SUE MCDONNELL

Harems *trekking* to water, with mares leading and stallions following

ELKANAH GROGAN

Jump

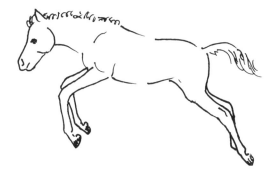

With mostly hind leg propulsion, moving forward with the forelegs leaving the ground first followed by the hind legs. Jumping can be vertical to clear high obstacles or broad to span ditches or small streams.

Described in:

Horses — semi-feral ponies (Tyler 1972); domestic and feral horses and ponies (Waring 1983)

Donkeys — feral asses *Equus africanus* (Moehlman 1974, 1998)

Play group foal *jumping*

Stampede

Running of a group together as a unit at high speed.

Described in:

Horses — domestic and feral horses and ponies (S McDonnell unpublished observations)

Zebra — Cape Mountain zebra *Equus zebra zebra* (Penzhorn 1994)

Herd *stampeding* away from intruder

Swim

Forward movement through water propelled by the legs in a trot motion. Head and nose are kept above the surface.

Comments: Horses may wade and swim routinely at deep watering sites (S McDonnell unpublished observations).

Described in:

Horses — domestic and feral horses and ponies (Waring 1983)

Przewalski horses — zoo-managed Przewalski horses (Boyd and Houpt 1994)

Two-year-old colt *swimming* in pond during spring heat wave

ELKANAH GROGAN

REST

Although horses can remain normally alert and active for days without lying down or falling asleep, both standing and recumbent rest typically occur several times throughout the day and night in unthreatened well-established groups of horses in familiar surroundings. A group within a herd tends to rest together.

Within a group, one or more individuals usually remain standing and more alert, serving as sentinels. Resting sites as well as the standing or lying position of the individuals typically appear to be selected for optimal detection of threats and rapid escape, with protection from weather and insects as a secondary factor.

Andre Dallaire's 1986 introductory review of the physiology and behavior of rest and sleep in equids is still quite current. When horses sleep, either standing or recumbent, they typically have a marked reduction in heart and respiratory rate. When in recumbent sleep, it is common for foals to have brief episodes of jerky leg movements, as if running. These "sleep running" episodes likely correspond to rapid eye movement (REM) or deep sleep.

Rest Standing

Standing inactive in a relaxed posture, usually with head slightly lowered, eyes partly or nearly closed, and often bearing weight on three legs (one hind leg slightly flexed). With deeper drowsiness (transition between wakefulness and sleep), the lips relax and the ears rotate laterally.

Described in:

Horses — domestic and feral horses and ponies (Feist 1971, Tyler 1972, Waring 1983, Keiper 1985)

Przewalski horses — zoo-managed Przewalski horses (Boyd and Houpt 1994)

Donkeys — feral asses *Equus africanus* (Moehlman 1974, 1998); feral asses *Equus asinus* (McCort 1980)

Zebra — Grevy's zebra *Equus grevyi* (Gardner 1983); Cape Mountain zebra *Equus zebra zebra* (Penzhorn 1984)

Mare *rests standing* over foal

Sleep Standing

With eyes closed and head lowered below the back, light sleep in a standing position.

Comments: Ligaments and tendons in the limbs and a check apparatus in the forelegs and reciprocal apparatus in the hind legs enable light standing sleep in equids (Dallaire 1986).

Described in:

Horses — domestic and feral horses and ponies (Waring 1983)

Przewalski horses — zoo-managed Przewalski horses (Boyd and Houpt 1994)

Donkeys — feral asses *Equus africanus* (Moehlman 1974, 1998); feral asses *Equus asinus* (McCort 1980)

Zebra — Grevy's zebra *Equus grevyi* (Gardner 1983)

SUE MCDONNELL

Harem *sleep standing*

Rest Recumbent

Lying Down

Getting Up

Sternal Recumbency

Lateral Recumbency

Rest or sleep while lying down with head up or with legs and head outstretched.

Comments: Deep sleep occurs only in recumbent sleep (Dallaire 1986).

Described in:

Horses — feral horses (Feist 1971); semi-feral ponies (Tyler 1972); free-ranging Appaloosa horses (Blakeslee 1974); feral horses (Boyd 1980); domestic and feral horses and ponies (Waring 1983); feral ponies (Keiper 1985)

Przewalski horses — zoo-managed Przewalski horses (Boyd and Houpt 1994)

Donkeys — feral asses *Equus africanus* (Moehlman 1974, 1998); feral asses *Equus asinus* (McCort 1980)

Zebra — Grevy's zebra *Equus grevyi* (Gardner 1983); Cape Mountain zebra *Equus zebra zebra* (Penzhorn 1984)

Entire harem *resting recumbent* **with one sentinel** *standing resting*

Sternal and lateral (inset) *recumbency*

Yawn

Deep, long inhalation with mouth widely opened, with jaws either directly opposed or moved from side to side.

Comments: Seen commonly in association with standing and recumbent rest and masturbation.

Described in:

Horses — feral horses (Feist 1971); semi-feral ponies (Tyler 1972); domestic and feral horses and ponies (Waring 1983)

Przewalski horses — zoo-managed Przewalski horses (Boyd and Houpt 1994)

Donkeys — feral asses *Equus africanus* (Moehlman 1974, 1998)

Zebra — Plains zebra *Equus burchelli* (S McDonnell unpublished observations)

Harem stallion *yawning*

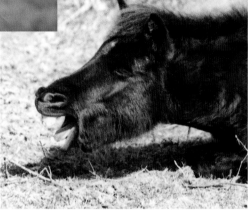

Yawn **while** *resting recumbent*

Resting yearling companions simultaneously *yawning*

Stretch

Rigid extension of the limbs and arching of the neck and back.

Other names: *pandiculation* (general animal behavior terminology).

Comments: In general animal behavior, considered a comfort behavior that may serve to increase muscle tone and circulation to the limb, particularly after rest (McFarland 1987).

Described in:

Horses — domestic and feral horses and ponies (Feist 1971, Tyler 1972, Waring 1983, Keiper 1985)

Przewalski horses — zoo-managed Przewalski horses (Boyd and Houpt 1994)

Donkeys — feral asses *Equus africanus* (Moehlman 1974, 1998)

Zebra — Plains zebra *Equus burchelli* (S McDonnell unpublished observations)

Foal *stretch* after *standing rest*

Bachelor *stretching* **after** *standing rest*

Harem stallion *stretching* **after** *standing rest*

Mare *stretching* **forelegs while** *recumbent resting* **after foaling**

GROOMING AND
INSECT CONTROL

A number of behaviors are directed at skin and coat care and insect control. These behaviors can be performed individually or with one or more cohorts. Depending upon the environment, a considerable portion of the daily time budget at certain times of the year can be consumed with grooming and insect avoidance (Duncan and Cowtan 1980; Keiper and Berger 1982). The examples included here are the most common seen in horses.

Roll

Dropping from standing to sternal recumbency, then rotating one or more times from sternal to dorsal recumbency, tucking the legs against the body.

Other names: *dust bathe* (feral asses, McCort 1980).

Comments: Common rolling sites are used repeatedly; with disruption of vegetation, they become barren and dusty.

Described in:

Horses — domestic and feral horses and ponies (Feist 1971, Tyler 1972, Waring 1983, Keiper 1985)

Przewalski horses — zoo-managed Przewalski horses (Boyd and Houpt 1994)

Donkeys — feral asses *Equus africanus* (Moehlman 1974, 1998); feral asses *Equus asinus* (McCort 1980)

Zebra — Grevy's zebra *Equus grevyi* (Gardner 1983); Cape Mountain zebra *Equus zebra zebra* (Penzhorn 1984)

Roll

Harem stallion
rolling **in**
muddy water

SUE MCDONNELL

Typical rolling sequence including dropping down (1), *rolling* (2), and *shaking* (3) on a community rolling bowl resulting from repeated use

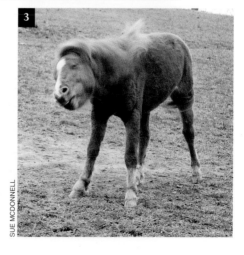

SUE MCDONNELL

63

Roll

Rolling and *drinking* during summer afternoon
excursion to pond

Typical rolling sequence including dropping down, *rolling*, and *shaking* on a community rolling bowl resulting from repeated use

ELKANAH GROGAN

Roll

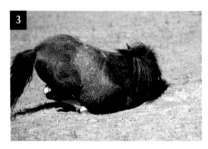

**Harem stallion rolling sequence
adjacent to pond during daily
excursion for *drinking* and
*rolling in water***

ELKANAH GROGAN

ELKANAH GROGAN

Shake

Rapid, rhythmic rotation of the head, neck, and upper body along the long axis while standing with feet planted.

Described in:

Horses — domestic and feral horses and ponies (Waring 1983)

Przewalski horses — zoo-managed Przewalski horses (Boyd and Houpt 1994)

Donkeys — feral asses *Equus africanus* (Moehlman 1974, 1998); feral asses *Equus asinus* (McCort 1980)

Zebra — Grevy's zebra *Equus grevyi* (Gardner 1983); Cape Mountain zebra *Equus zebra zebra* (Penzhorn 1984)

Assistant harem stallion
shaking after *rolling*

ELKANAH GROGAN

Autogroom

Autogroom

Nibbling, biting, licking, or rubbing a part of the body.

Other names: *rub, scratch* (Waring 1983).

Described in:

Horses — feral horses (Feist 1971, Keiper 1985); domestic and feral horses and ponies (Waring 1983)

Przewalski horses — zoo-managed Przewalski horses (Boyd and Houpt 1994)

Donkeys — feral asses *Equus africanus* (Moehlman 1974, 1998); feral asses *Equus asinus* (McCort 1980)

Zebra — Cape Mountain zebra *Equus zebra zebra* (Penzhorn 1984)

**Neonate *autogrooming* flank
with mouth**

**Yearling *autogrooming* foreleg
with mouth**

Yearling *autogrooming* crest of neck and ear with hoof

**Recumbent neonatal colt *autogrooming* groin
with mouth**

Mutual Groom

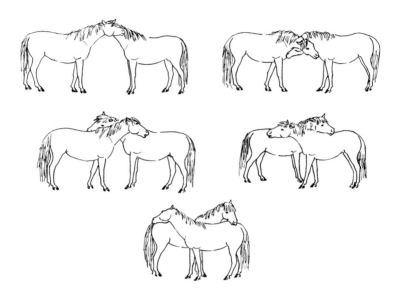

Herd mates standing beside one another, usually head-to-shoulder or head-to-tail, grooming each other's neck, mane, chest, back, rump, or tail by gentle nipping, nuzzling, or rubbing.

Other names: *allogrooming* (McFarland 1987).

Comments: Appears to serve as an aid for shedding, parasite control, stress alleviation, and social bonding. Research indicates that stimulation of the natural grooming sites is especially calming to the horse (Feh and de Mazières 1993).

Described in:

Horses — feral horses (Feist 1971); semi-feral ponies (Tyler 1972); feral ponies (Keiper 1985)

Przewalski horses — zoo-managed Przewalski horses (Boyd and Houpt 1994)

Donkeys — feral asses *Equus africanus* (Moehlman 1974, 1998); feral asses *Equus asinus* (McCort 1980)

Zebra — Cape Mountain zebra *Equus zebra zebra* (Penzhorn 1984)

**Yearling colt grooming dam's crest of neck while
she grooms his chest**

Foal *mutual grooming* dam

**Harem stallion and mare
*mutual grooming***

73

Swish/Swat Insects

Swish the tail, swing the head against the shoulder or abdomen, flex the chin to the chest, or flex a limb to remove insects.

Other names: *tail switching* (Waring 1983); *tail swishing*; *tail lashing* (Hafez et al. 1962).

Described in:

Horses — domestic and feral horses and ponies (Waring 1983)

Przewalski horses — zoo-managed Przewalski horses (Boyd and Houpt 1994)

Donkeys — feral asses *Equus africanus* (Moehlman 1974, 1998)

Zebra — Cape Mountain zebra *Equus zebra zebra* (Penzhorn 1984); Plains zebra *Equus burchelli* (S McDonnell unpublished observations)

Mare and foal swishing tails to *swat* flies

AMY POULIN

***Swatting* flies with a hind leg flexed against the abdomen**

ELKANAH GROGAN

Stamp

Sharply strike the ground with a hoof by flexing and raising and then rapidly lowering a fore or hind leg.

Other names: stomp.

Described in:

Horses — domestic and feral horses and ponies (Waring 1983)

Przewalski horses — zoo-managed Przewalski horses (Boyd and Houpt 1994)

Donkeys — feral asses *Equus africanus* (Moehlman 1974, 1998); feral asses *Equus asinus* (McCort 1980)

Zebra — Cape Mountain zebra *Equus zebra zebra* (Penzhorn 1984)

Colt *stamping* flies while loafing

Insect Control — Mutual

While standing head-to-tail within close proximity, two or more animals swish their tails, effectively removing insects from the head and hindquarters of the participants.

Described in:

Horses — domestic and feral horses and ponies (Waring 1983)

Przewalski horses — zoo-managed Przewalski horses (Boyd and Houpt 1994)

Donkeys — feral asses *Equus africanus* (Moehlman 1974, 1998)

Zebra — Cape Mountain zebra *Equus zebra zebra* (Penzhorn 1984)

Harem stallion and mare sharing tails

SHELTER AND
COMFORT SEEKING

Animals seek shelter and relief from insects, sun and heat, cold, wind, and storms. Horses are known for their adaptability to a wide range of environmental conditions. This includes the physiological capacity to adapt, such as hair coat variation and other thermoregulatory mechanisms. Behavior also plays an obvious role in the ability to thrive under various and even widely changing conditions and environments. An interesting comparison of such behavior of horses in island and desert environments has been reported by Ron Keiper and Joel Berger (1982). Included here are common examples of such shelter and comfort-seeking behavior of horses.

Backs to Natural Windbreak

Standing alone, or in groups, taking advantage of natural windbreaks of vegetation or terrain.

Described in:

Horses — domestic and feral horses and ponies (Waring 1983)

Przewalski horses — zoo-managed Przewalski horses (Boyd and Houpt 1994)

Donkeys — feral asses *Equus africanus* (Moehlman 1974, 1998)

Zebra — Cape Mountain zebra *Equus zebra zebra* (Penzhorn 1984)

Shelter formed by ponies browsing out multiflora rose doorway (In view is the harem stallion guarding the door while the mares and young are resting under the hedge.)

Backs to Weather

During heavy rain or wind, standing or grazing oriented with the hindquarters into the wind.

Comments: Serves to reduce area of body exposure and minimize heat loss.

Described in:

Horses — domestic and feral horses and ponies (Waring 1983)

Przewalski horses — zoo-managed Przewalski horses (Boyd and Houpt 1994)

Donkeys — feral asses *Equus africanus* (Moehlman 1974, 1998)

Zebra — Cape Mountain zebra *Equus zebra zebra* (Penzhorn 1984)

Huddle

Two or more herd mates standing closely together. During calm, the individuals are typically standing or lying in the same orientation, as shown in *backs to weather* and *backs to natural windbreak*. During alarm, herd mates are usually oriented with individuals facing and alert to various directions. Foals are typically "inside the huddle."

Described in:

Horses — feral horses and ponies (Keiper 1985)
Donkeys — semi-feral donkeys (J Beech unpublished observations)

Harem band *huddling*

Sunning

Resting or *standing resting* in sunny warm areas during cold weather.

Other names: *basking.*
Described in:
Horses — domestic and feral horses and ponies (Waring 1983)
Zebra — Cape Mountain zebra *Equus zebra zebra* (Penzhorn 1984)

SUE MCDONNELL

Bachelors *sunning* and *resting*

Stand/Rest in Water

Stand for long periods (up to hours) or lie sternal or recumbent in knee-high or shallower water.

Other names: *wading while drinking* (Cape Mountain zebra, Penzhorn 1984).

Described in:

Horses — feral ponies (Keiper 1985)

Zebra — Cape Mountain zebra *Equus zebra zebra* (Penzhorn 1984)

Bachelor *standing in water*

SUE MCDONNELL

Mares *standing in water*

AMY POULIN

Mare *resting sternal* **in water**

INVESTIGATION

Horses, as with any mammalian species, encounter situations in which their behavior clearly indicates what we would call investigation. When encountering novel objects, odors, or a newborn addition to the group, their behavior typically involves exposing the various sensory modalities to the stimuli. Most situations suggesting investigation often involve a cluster of looking, smelling, mouthing, pawing, and tasting, and, therefore, access to visual, olfactory (smell), tactile (touch), and gustatory (taste) information. The behavior usually commences in a tentative manner and can take various physical postures and temporal associations depending upon the specific situation. Some of the commonly observed specific investigatory responses of horses are detailed in this section.

Sniff

With nose near object of interest, draw air in through nostrils.

Other names: *smell* (Waring 1983).

Described in:

Horses — domestic and feral horses and ponies (Waring 1983)

Przewalski horses — zoo-managed Przewalski horses (Boyd and Houpt 1994)

Donkeys — feral asses *Equus africanus* (Moehlman 1974, 1998)

Zebra — Cape Mountain zebra *Equus zebra zebra* (Penzhorn 1984)

Group *sniffing* novel object

Mouth

Manipulate with open mouth, as if to gain touch or taste.

Described in:

Horses — domestic and feral horses and ponies (Waring 1983)

Przewalski horses — zoo-managed Przewalski horses (Boyd and Houpt 1994)

Donkeys — feral asses *Equus africanus* (Moehlman 1974, 1998)

Mature stallion *mouthing* thistle

Lick

Contact an object with the tongue.

Described in:

Horses — domestic and feral horses and ponies (Waring 1983)

Przewalski horses — zoo-managed Przewalski horses (Boyd and Houpt 1994)

Donkeys — feral asses *Equus africanus* (Moehlman 1974, 1998)

Paw

With an object as an apparent target, a foreleg is lifted off the ground slightly, extended quickly in a forward direction, and followed by a backward, toe-dragging movement as if digging.

Described in:

Horses — domestic and feral horses and ponies (Waring 1983)

Przewalski horses — zoo-confined Przewalski horses (S McDonnell unpublished observations)

Donkeys — feral asses *Equus africanus* (Moehlman 1974, 1998); feral asses *Equus asinus* (McCort 1980)

Zebra — Cape Mountain zebra *Equus zebra zebra* (Penzhorn 1984)

Male foal *pawing* salt lick

Masturbation

Spontaneous Erection and Penile Movements

Penile erection with rhythmic drawing of the penis against the abdomen, with or without pelvic thrusting.

Other names: *extraneous penis extension* (Penzhorn 1984).

Comments: Occurs in males of all ages in both solitary or social settings, while *resting, grazing,* or *standing alert*. Episodes typically last about three minutes and occur at about 90-minute intervals. Ejaculation is rare (McDonnell et al. 1991).

Described in:

Horse — domestic and feral horses and ponies (Feist 1971, Tyler 1972, Waring 1983, Keiper 1985)

Przewalski horses — zoo-managed Przewalski horses (Boyd and Houpt 1994)

Bachelor stallions *masturbating* while grazing

Donkey — feral asses *Equus africanus* (Moehlman 1974, 1998); semi-feral donkeys (Henry et al. 1991)

Zebra — Grevy's zebra *Equus grevyi* (Gardner 1983); Cape Mountain zebra *Equus zebra zebra* (Penzhorn 1984)

SECTION II

GENERAL SOCIAL COMMUNICATION

Horses are known for their multi-sensory alertness, herd vigilance, and instantaneous reactivity to threat. Postures and expressions in various combinations appear to be important visual elements of communication. Within and between bands of horses, very subtle changes in ear or tail position appear to convey information. Horses emit a variety of vocalizations as well as other sounds that are likely to serve as communication within the herd. These include specific vocalizations, such as whinnies and neighs, snorts, squeals, and grunts. Horses also groan and sigh, and these sounds also sometimes appear to be perceived by herd mates. Hoof sounds, from pawing, stamping, or contact with the substrate during locomotion, also appear to communicate information among horses.

Chemical cues also likely play a large part in communication within and between groups of horses, as well as in perception of threatening predators. Stallions display conspicuous elimination and marking behavior sequences in which long periods seem devoted to sniffing excretions of herd mates and of fecal pile accumulations of stallions from competing groups within a large herd. Whenever herd mates or strangers meet, they almost always approach nose to nose with deliberate sniffing of one another's exhaled breath. Many observers have speculated that breath may carry information about relatedness or status.

Among closely bonded band members, particularly mares and their foals, tactile communication no doubt is important. An interesting behavior that likely includes elements of communication is mutual grooming. Two horses stand facing one another, nibbling insects or tufts of shedding coat from the neck or back of a partner. In addition to obvious grooming needs, this behavior may communicate trust and bonding among participants. Mutual grooming among bachelor stallions or among youngsters often precedes play bouts. So it is believed to be a play-initiation behavior.

Established order of dominance and submission is important in the social order within and between groups of a herd. With an established order, overt fighting is reduced and competition seems to be settled with simple threats and retreats. Horses are an open plains species, so an important element of avoiding fights is simple retreat from the threat. Dominant individuals can effectively direct the movement of other animals or can control a limited resource with a simple head toss threat or threat gaze that involves a stare with the ears held back and the head lowered.

Equids interact to a limited extent with other species in their habitat. In particular, communication of calm and alarm appears to transfer among species. Although not common, both adults and young can occasionally be seen interacting playfully or aggressively with small mammals and birds. A horse may chase a ground hog or fox pup. And sometimes horses are chased or herded away by other species. For example, in our semi-feral herd we sometimes see ground-nesting birds chase a pony from the vicinity of their clutch or young.

This section includes the most common head postures and facial expressions, greeting postures, and vocalizations. It also includes examples of interspecies interactions.

Head Postures and Facial Expressions

Relaxed Contentment

Curious Alert

Dozy

Asleep

Fear

Fear/Mild Threat

Threat

Eye Rolling

Head Postures and Facial Expressions

Relaxed and *drowsy* expression in a mare

Curiously alert foal

Eye-rolling expression in stallions play fighting

Threat Postures

Bite Threat

Kick Threat

Stallion *kick threat* to approaching harem stallion

Mare mild *head threat*

Submissive Retreat

Movement that maintains or increases an individual's distance from an approaching or following herd mate. The head is usually held low and ears turned back. The retreat can be at any gait but typically occurs at the trot.

Other names: *facing away* (Feist 1971), *leaving* (zebra, Schilder and Boer 1987), *avoidance behavior* (zebra, Schilder 1990), *fleeing* (Houpt and Wolski 1982), *passive reaction* (Syme and Syme 1979).

Described in:

Horses — feral horses and ponies (Miller 1981, Keiper 1985)

Przewalski horses — zoo-managed Przewalski horses (Feh 1988, S McDonnell unpublished observations)

Donkeys — feral asses *Equus africanus* (Moehlman 1974, 1998); feral asses *Equus asinus* (McCort 1980)

Zebra — semi-captive Plains zebra *Equus burchelli* (Schilder 1990)

Yearling *retreating* from a harem stallion

Infant-like Submissive Posture

Opening and closing of the jaw (see *snapping*, p. 116, 225) with head lowered and extended in nursing posture and body lowered by bending of the knees and hunching of the hindquarters.

Described in:

Horses — domestic and feral horses and ponies (Feist 1971, Wells and Von Goldschmidt-Rothschild 1979, Keiper 1985)

Przewalski horses — zoo-managed Przewalski horses (Feh 1988, Hogan et al. 1988, Boyd and Houpt 1994)

Donkeys — feral asses *Equus africanus* (Moehlman 1974, 1998); feral asses *Equus asinus* (McCort 1980); domestic donkeys (S McDonnell unpublished observations)

Zebra — semi-captive Plains zebra *Equus burchelli* (Schilder et al. 1984)

Snapping and dropping low of *infant-like submissive posture* of a two-year-old colt to harem stallion

Shying

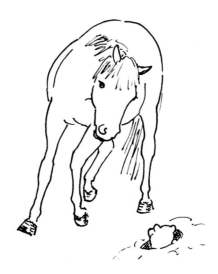

Sudden veering to avoid novel or fear-provoking animate or inanimate stimulus.

Other names: *spook.*
Described in:
Horses — domestic horses and ponies (McBane 1987)

Few-days-old colt *shying* as he runs toward dam

Vocalization and Auditory Communication

Horses and Ponies

Excellent descriptions of vocalizations and sounds of horses, including sonograms, are provided by Waring (1983). The following brief summaries are based on Waring's descriptions.

Whinny (neigh): loud, prolonged call, typically of 1 to 3 seconds, beginning high pitched and ending lower pitched. The head is elevated and the mouth slightly opened during the *whinny*. The *whinny* is associated with *alert* and *approach* from a distance, usually between an affiliated pair, and usually followed by a relatively friendly or playful interaction as opposed to frank aggressive encounter.

Nicker: low-pitched, gutturally pulsated vocalization that occurs most frequently in a mother to her foal and in a stallion during quiet precopulatory interaction with a mare. The character of the *nicker* varies with the excitement of the situation.

Squeal: high-pitched vocalization of variable loudness and typically of less than 1 second. The head can be in a variety of positions, and the mouth is typically closed during the *squeal*. These vocalizations are typical during *olfactory investigation*, *posturing*, *biting*, and *nipping* as well as during both mock and serious fighting.

Scream: of similar high pitch, but louder and longer than the squeal. Associated with the same situations as *squeal*, but typically with more serious aggression.

Snort: sound produced upon forceful quick exhalation of less than 1 second duration. Associated with *olfactory investigation*, *prancing*, *posturing*, and close combat involving *rearing*, *boxing*, *kneeling*, and *circling*.

Grunt: low-pitched vocalization of about 0.5 seconds. The mouth is closed during the *grunt*. As with the *snort*, the *grunt* is associated with *olfactory investigation*, *posturing*, and close combat involving *rearing*, *boxing*, *kneeling*, and *circling*.

Blow: sound produced upon strong, sharp exhalation. In startle situations appears to communicate alarm to herd mates.

Groan: monotone hum-like sound produced during exhalation, typically lasting up to 2 seconds. *Groans* most commonly occur during discomfort in recumbent animals, for example during parturition. Some individuals also normally emit a short *groan* or *sigh* upon lying down.

Sigh: audible prolonged loud exhalation following quick deep inhalation.

Stallion *squealing* during posturing

Bachelor *whinnying* as approaching a cohort bachelor

Bachelor *whinnying*

Screaming whinny of a young bachelor approaching cohorts

Other Sounds Produced that May Serve as Acoustical Signals

Examples

Hoof beats	**Grazing**	**Tail swishing**
Coughing, sneezing, snorting	**Sniffing**	**Grooming**
Sucking	**Snapping**	**Snoring**
Splashing in Water	**Flattus**	**Copulation**

Socially Facilitated Behaviors

Behavior that appears to be stimulated or triggered by its occurrence in one or more other nearby conspecifics (members of the same species). In equids, behaviors such as *grazing*, *resting*, *play*, *investigation*, *grooming*, *rolling*, and *yawning* often occur simultaneously and so appear to be socially facilitated.

Other names: contagious behavior.
Described in:
Horses — feral horses and ponies (Blakeslee 1974, Keiper 1985, Rifa 1990)

Socially facilitated *alert* among young bachelor cohorts

Herd mates simultaneously *grazing* while *nursing* their foals

Socially facilitated *grazing* involving multiple bands of a herd

Socially facilitated aggression in a young foal following dam in *head threatening* cohort over limited resource (salt block)

ELKANAH GROGAN

Interspecies Interactions

Apparent recognition and communication or interaction with animals of other species.

Other names: *extra-specific interaction.*

Described in:

Horses — semi-feral pony adults displace domestic cattle, foals play with domestic cattle calves, and co-graze with deer on managed forest reserve (Tyler 1972); feral ponies and birds forage together (Keiper 1985); semi-feral ponies and white-tailed deer co-react to alarm signals (S McDonnell unpublished observations); semi-feral ponies herding and herded by Canadian geese (S McDonnell unpublished observations); semi-feral ponies playing "cat and mouse" games with ground hogs (S McDonnell unpublished observations)

Zebra — Cape Mountain zebra *Equus zebra zebra* react with alarm signals of other hoofstock such as antelope, eland, black wildebeest, gemsbok; red-winged starling and pied crows associate with Cape Mountain zebra herds (Penzhorn 1984)

Small native Pennsylvania bird foraging insects stirred up by the grazing trio (Note the foal's ears focused *alert* to the bird as it lands on a mare.)

SECTION III
INTERMALE INTERACTION

For horses living in natural social units, interactions among stallions comprise a prominent feature of social behavior. Interactions among bachelors range from peaceful and cooperative to sparring. The ongoing sparring may be fiercely competitive, but it rarely appears to inflict injury. Interactions between harem stallions or between harem stallions and bachelors again vary from peaceful ritual-like interactions to a severely frank aggressive type where there appears to be no "holding back" or sporting tone. Together, the incessant bachelor sparring and the serious intermale encounters account for much of the visual action and the majority of the vocalizations and other sounds  of a herd of horses. But equally fascinating are the quiet interactions among bachelors of an established band reflecting close bonds and the companionship among stallions within a bachelor band.

This section includes the most common behaviors of ongoing intermale agonistic interaction. Further discussion and illustration of intermale interaction within the context of establishing and maintaining a harem are included in Section IV on Reproductive Behavior.

Alert

Rigid stance with the neck elevated and the head oriented toward the object or animal of focus. The ears are held stiffly upright and forward, and the nostrils may be slightly dilated.

Other names: *stand-stare* (Feist 1971), *stare* (Waring 1983), *standing alert* (Duncan 1985), *vigilance* (Berger 1986), *attention face* (zebra, Schilder and Boer 1987), and, if the animal turns the body to face the object of interest, *turn toward* (asses, McCort 1980).

Comments: The whinny vocalization may accompany this stance. *Alert* posture may be followed by approach, followed by either friendly or aggressive interactions, or by resumption of the previous activity. Waring (1983) described *alarm* as a stronger form of the *alert* stance, with eyes widely open and sclera showing. The behavior may include an arched neck and flared nostrils.

Described in:

Horses — feral horses (Feist 1971)

Przewalski horses — zoo-managed Przewalski horses (Boyd and Houpt 1994)

Donkeys — feral asses *Equus africanus* (Moehlman 1974, 1998); feral asses *Equus asinus* (McCort 1980)

Zebra — Plains zebra *Equus burchelli* (MBH Schilder personal communication 1992)

Semi-solitary bachelor *alert*

Bachelor group *alert* to intruders

ELKANAH GROGAN

Approach

Forward movement at any gait toward another stallion in a straight or curving path. The head may be elevated and ears forward or the head may be lowered and ears pinned back (see also herding and head threat).

Other names: *walk toward* or *run toward* (asses, McCort 1980).

Comments: *Approach* necessarily precedes most close agonistic interactions. First close contact of males is typically nose-to-nose, as it is for general intra-species approach. One stallion may approach another, or two stallions may simultaneously approach each other. Also, stallions may approach others to form larger assemblies. *Approach* may be followed immediately by retreat of a stallion being approached or by olfactory investigation or fighting, which may evolve into a chase.

Described in:

Horses — domestic and feral horses and ponies (Welsh 1975, Waring 1983)

Przewalski horses — zoo-managed Przewalski horses (Feh 1988, Boyd and Houpt 1994)

Donkeys — feral asses *Equus africanus* (Moehlman 1974, 1998); feral asses *Equus asinus* (McCort 1980)

Zebra — Cape Mountain zebra *Equus zebra zebra* (Penzhorn 1984); semi-captive Plains zebra *Equus burchelli* (Schilder 1988, 1990)

Harem stallions *approaching*

Approach **and** *olfactory investigation* **among stallions of a small bachelor band**

Arched Neck Threat

Neck tightly flexed with the muzzle drawn toward the chest.

Other names: *arched neck* (Berger 1986).

Comments: *Arched neck threats* are components of most male-male interactions (Miller 1981). These threats may be displayed concurrently with or as a component of other behaviors, for example *posturing, parallel prance, pawing, olfactory investigation, strike threat. Arched neck threats* are observed during close aggressive encounters and ritualized interactions.

Described in:

Horses — feral horses (Miller 1981, Berger 1986)

Przewalski — zoo-managed Przewalski horses (Boyd and Houpt 1994)

Zebra — has not been observed in zebras (MBH Schilder personal communication 1991)

Harem stallion threatening an intruder at water crossing

JEN PLEBANI

Ears Laid Back/Pinned

Ears pressed caudally against the head and neck. Typically associated with intense aggressive interaction.

Other names: *ears retracted* (Berger 1986).

Described in:

Horses — domestic and feral horses and ponies (Feist 1971, Waring 1983, Berger 1986)

Przewalski horses — zoo-managed Przewalski horses (Keiper 1988, Boyd and Houpt 1994)

Donkeys — Asiatic wild asses *Equus hemionus* (Bannikov 1971); feral asses *Equus africanus* (Moehlman 1974, 1998); feral asses *Equus asinus* (McCort 1980)

Zebra — semi-captive Plains zebra *Equus burchelli* (Schilder et al. 1984)

**Harem stallion with *ears laid back*
to nearby bachelors**

Head Threat

Head lowered with the ears pinned, neck stretched or extended toward the target stallion, and, often, the lips pursed. The pointing extension of the head and neck may be interrupted with momentary tossing, rotating gestures of the head.

Other names: *head extension* (Waring 1983), *head swing* (Feist 1971), and when gesturing of the head and neck, *head toss* (Berger 1986).

Described in:

Horses — domestic and feral horses and ponies (Wells and Von Goldschmidt-Rothschild 1979, Waring 1983)

Przewalski horses — zoo-managed Przewalski horses (Feh 1988, Boyd and Houpt 1994)

Donkeys — Asiatic wild asses *Equus hemionus* (Bannikov 1971); feral asses *Equus africanus* (Moehlman 1974, 1998); feral asses *Equus asinus* (McCort 1980)

Zebra — Cape Mountain *Equus zebra zebra* (Penzhorn 1984)

Harem stallion in *head threat* posture

Stomp

Raising and lowering of a foreleg to strike the ground sharply, usually repeatedly. *Stomping* differs from *pawing* in that *stomping* is a vertical rather than horizontal movement of the leg.

Other names: *stamp* (Welsh 1975, Waring 1983), *front hoof beating* (Hoffmann 1985).

Comments: *Stomping* is most commonly seen during posturing and ritualized interactive sequences. Waring (1983) interpreted forceful contact with the ground as an auditory signal.

Described in:

Horses — domestic and feral horses and ponies (Welsh 1975, Berger 1977, Waring 1983)

Przewalski horses — zoo-managed Przewalski horses (Boyd and Houpt 1994)

Donkeys — Asiatic wild asses *Equus hemionus* (Bannikov 1971); feral asses *Equus africanus* (Moehlman 1974, 1998); feral asses *Equus asinus* (McCort 1980)

Zebra — Plains zebra *Equus quagga* (Klingel 1967)

Stallions meeting with simultaneous *stomping*

113

Avoidance/Retreat

Movement that maintains or increases an individual's distance from an approaching stallion. The head is usually held low and ears turned back. The retreat can be at any gait but typically occurs at the trot.

Other names: *facing away* (Feist 1971), *leaving* (zebra, Schilder and Boer 1987), *avoidance behavior* (zebra, Schilder 1990), *fleeing* (Houpt and Wolski 1982), *passive reaction* (Syme and Syme 1979).

Comments: Waring (1983) used *flight* to refer to group retreat.

Described in:

Horses — feral horses (Miller 1981)

Przewalski horses—zoo-managed Przewalski horses (S McDonnell unpublished observations)

Donkeys — feral asses *Equus africanus* (Moehlman 1974, 1998); feral asses *Equus asinus* (McCort 1980)

Zebra — semi-captive Plains zebra *Equus burchelli* (Schilder 1990)

Young bachelor *retreating* from harem stallion

Follow

Move along behind another stallion, usually at the same gait as the stallion being followed. In contrast to a *chase*, there seems to be no attempt to direct the movement, attack, or overtake the leading stallion.

Described in:

Horses — domestic horses and ponies (Waring 1983)
Przewalski horses — zoo-managed Przewalski horses (Feh 1988)
Donkeys — feral asses *Equus africanus* (Moehlman 1974, 1998)
Zebra — semi-captive Plains zebra *Equus burchelli* (Schilder 1990)

Olfactory investigation **(1),** *posturing* **(2),** and *following* **(3) by harem stallion and assistant harem stallion of another harem band**

ELKANAH GROGAN

Snapping

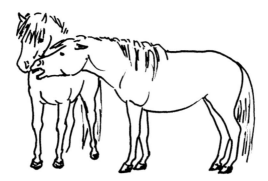

Moving the lower jaw up and down in a chewing or suckling motion, usually with the mouth open and lips drawn back exposing the incisors. A sucking sound may be made as the tongue is drawn against the roof of the mouth (Waring 1983). Typically, the head and neck are extended, with the ears relaxed and oriented back or laterally. This behavior is usually performed while approaching the head of another, usually on an angle.

Other names: *champing* (Wolski et al. 1980), *teeth-clapping* (Feist 1971), *tooth-clapping* (Boyd 1980; Przewalski horse, Feh 1988), *bared-teeth face* (zebra, Schilder and Boer 1987), *Unterlegenheitsgebarde* (Zeeb 1959), *jaw-waving* (Blakeslee 1974), and *jawing* (asses, Moehlman 1974, 1998; McCort 1980).

Comments: The name *snapping* was first used by Tyler (1972). It is commonly viewed as a submissive behavior because it is mostly observed when a submissive or young stallion approaches an older or more dominant stallion and because a similar behavior has been noted in foals when approaching adults. Boyd (1980) concluded that snapping does not inhibit aggression by others but instead may serve to calm the submissive individual. Crowell-Davis and her colleagues (1985) suggested that snapping may be a "displacement activity developed from nursing." A similar behavior, commonly called *jawing*, occurs at estrus in asses.

Described in:

Horses — domestic and feral horses and ponies (Feist 1971, Wells and Von Goldschmidt-Rothschild 1979)

Przewalski horses — zoo-managed Przewalski horses (Feh 1988, Hogan et al. 1988, Boyd and Houpt 1994)

Donkeys — feral asses *Equus africanus* (Moehlman 1974, 1998); feral asses *Equus asinus* (McCort 1980); semi-feral donkeys (S McDonnell unpublished observations)

Zebra — semi-captive Plains zebra *Equus burchelli* (Schilder et al. 1984)

Yearling *snapping* to mature stallion

Yearling *snapping* to mature stallion breeding

Head Bowing

Head bowing is a repeated, exaggerated, rhythmic flexing of the neck such that the muzzle is brought toward the point of the breast. Head bowing usually occurs synchronously between two stallions when they first approach each other head to head.

Described in:

Horses — semi-feral ponies (McDonnell and Haviland 1995)

Zebra — semi-wild Plains zebra *Equus burchelli* (MBH Schilder personal communication 1991).

Olfactory Investigation

Olfactory investigation involves sniffing various parts of another stallion's head and/or body. This behavior typically begins after stallions have approached one another nose to nose. After mutually sniffing face to face, typically one stallion works his way caudally along the other's body length, sniffing any or all of the following: neck, withers, flank, genitals, and tail or perineal region. During the investigation, it is common for one or both stallions to squeal, snort, kick threat, strike threat, or bite threat.

Other names: *social investigation* (Feh 1988), *genital inspection* (Schilder 1988), *inspection* (Schilder 1990).

Comments: Genital sniffing is a prominent aspect of the investigation.

Described in:

Horses — feral horses and ponies (Welsh 1975, McCort 1984)

Przewalski horses — zoo-managed Przewalski horses (Feh 1988, Boyd and Houpt 1994)

ELKANAH GROGAN

Harem stallion *sniffing* groin of bachelor

Donkeys — feral asses *Equus africanus* (Moehlman 1974, 1998); feral asses *Equus asinus* (McCort 1980)

Zebra — semi-captive Plains zebra *Equus burchelli* (Schilder 1990)

Posturing

Pre-fight head-bowing, prancing, stomping, olfactory investigation, as well as a stiffening of the entire body, including forelegs. The *arched neck threat* is also a major component, being held throughout most of the interaction. The participants may rub and push against one another.

Comments: Waring (1983) described the ears as forward and the tail elevated during much of the *posturing*.

Described in:

Horses — domestic and feral horses and ponies (Feist 1971, Welsh 1975, Berger 1977, Waring 1983)

Przewalski — zoo-managed Przewalski horses (Boyd and Houpt 1994)

Donkeys — feral asses *Equus africanus* (Moehlman 1974, 1998); feral asses *Equus asinus* (McCort 1980)

Zebra — Cape Mountain zebra *Equus zebra zebra* (Penzhorn 1984)

Assistant harem stallion and harem stallion *posturing*

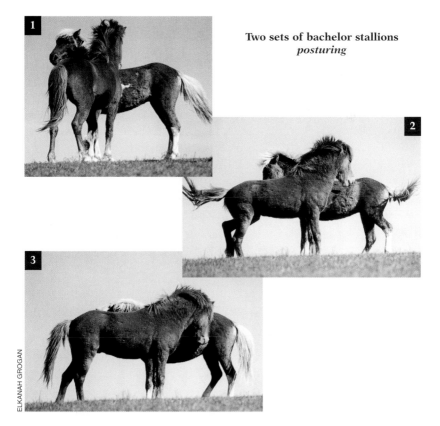

Two sets of bachelor stallions
posturing

ELKANAH GROGAN

Posturing

Bachelor stallions
posturing

SUE MCDONNELL

Parallel Prance

Two stallions, moving forward beside one another, shoulder-to-shoulder with arched necks and heads held high and ears forward, typically in a high-stepping, slow-cadenced trot (*passage*, in dressage terminology). Rhythmic snorts may accompany each stride. *Parallel prancing* often immediately precedes aggressive encounters. Solitary prancing also occurs.

Comments: Most often seen in neighboring harem stallions but also sometimes among bachelors or between a bachelor and harem stallion.

Described in:

Horses — domestic and feral horses (Feist 1971, Berger 1977, Waring 1983)

Przewalski — zoo-managed Przewalski horses (Boyd and Houpt 1994)

Bachelors *parallel prancing*

Head on Neck, Back, or Rump

Chin or entire head resting on top of the neck, body, or rump of another stallion. Often precedes a *mount*.

Described in:

Horses — feral horses (Feist 1971)

Przewalski horses — zoo-managed Przewalski horses (Boyd and Houpt 1994)

Donkeys — feral asses *Equus asinus* (McCort 1980)

Zebra — semi-captive Plains zebra *Equus burchelli* (Schilder 1988)

Young harem stallion with *head on back* of former bachelor cohort

Mutual Grooming

While standing beside one another, usually head-to-shoulder or head-to-tail, two (or rarely more) partners groom each other's neck, mane, rump, or tail by gentle nipping, nuzzling, or rubbing. For males, almost always among bachelors or between a harem stallion and a son still living within the natal band.

Comments: In Przewalski horses, mutual grooming is reportedly more common among younger bachelors (Hoffmann 1985).

Described in:

Horses — feral horses (Feist 1971, Wells and Von Goldschmidt-Rothschild 1988)

Przewalski horses — zoo-managed Przewalski horses (Hoffman 1985, Hogan et al. 1988)

Donkeys — feral asses *Equus africanus* (Moehlman 1974, 1998);

feral asses *Equus asinus* (McCort 1980)

Zebra — Cape Mountain zebra *Equus zebra zebra* (Penzhorn 1984); semi-captive Plains zebra *Equus burchelli* (Schilder 1990)

***Mutual grooming* by bachelor stallions during springtime shedding**

ELKANAH GROGAN

Rolling

Dropping from standing to sternal recumbency, then rotating one or more times from sternal to dorsal recumbency, tucking the legs against the body. *Rolling* typically occurs on dusty or sandy areas. *Rolling* is usually preceded by pawing and nosing of the ground and followed by body shaking. Snort vocalizations may occur when the stallion is nosing the ground or shaking.

Described in:

Horses — domestic horses and ponies (Waring 1983)

Przewalski horses — zoo-managed Przewalski horses (Boyd and Houpt 1994)

Donkeys — feral asses *Equus asinus* (McCort 1980); semi-feral donkeys (S McDonnell unpublished observations)

Zebra — semi-captive Plains zebra *Equus burchelli* (MBH Schilder personal communication 1991)

Yearling and stallion *rolling*

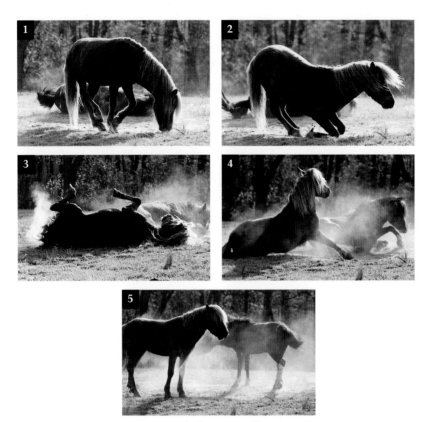

Bachelor pair *rolling*

Rolling **and elimination marking site**

Lunge

Swift forward thrust of the body from the rear position or charge from close range toward another stallion (usually toward his fore body), most often displayed concurrently with a bite threat, with ears pinned.

Other names: *attacking* (Schilder 1988).

Described in:

Horses — semi-feral ponies (McDonnell and Haviland 1995)

Przewalski horses — zoo-confined Przewalski horses (S McDonnell unpublished observations)

Donkeys — feral asses *Equus africanus* (Moehlman 1974, 1998); feral asses *Equus asinus* (McCort 1980)

Zebra — Cape Mountain zebra *Equus zebra zebra* (Penzhorn 1984); semi-captive Plains zebra *Equus burchelli* (Schilder 1988)

Bachelor *lunging* toward assistant harem stallion

Balk

Abrupt halt or reversal of direction with movement of the head and neck in a rapid, sweeping, dorsolateral motion away from an apparent threat while the hind legs remain stationary. The forelegs may simultaneously lift off the ground. Typically associated with an approach or lunge of another stallion.

Described in:

Horses — ponies (McDonnell and Haviland 1995)

Przewalski horses — zoo-managed Przewalski horses (KA Houpt videotaped observations)

Donkeys — feral asses *Equus africanus* (Moehlman 1974, 1998); feral asses *Equus asinus* (McCort 1980)

Zebra — Cape Mountain zebra *Equus zebra zebra* (Penzhorn 1984)

Simultaneous *balk* during harem stallion encounter

Head Bump

A rapid lateral toss of the head that forcefully contacts the head and neck of another stallion. Usually the eyes remain closed and the ears forward.

Other names: *head swing* (Feist 1971).

Described in:

Horses — domestic and feral horses (Feist 1971, Syme and Syme 1979)

Przewalski — zoo-managed Przewalski horses (KA Houpt videotaped observations)

Donkeys — feral asses *Equus africanus* (Moehlman 1974, 1998); feral asses *Equus asinus* (McCort 1980)

Zebra — Cape Mountain zebra *Equus zebra zebra* (Penzhorn 1984)

SUE MCDONNELL

Head bump **in bachelor interaction**

Push

Pressing of the head, neck, shoulder, chest, body, or rump against another in an apparent attempt to displace or pin the target stallion against an object.

Other names: *bumping* (Waring 1983).

Described in:

Horses — domestic and feral horses and ponies (Feist 1971, Waring 1983)

Przewalski horses — zoo-managed Przewalski horses (KA Houpt videotaped observations)

Donkeys — feral asses *Equus africanus* (Moehlman 1974, 1998); feral asses *Equus asinus* (McCort 1980)

Zebra — semi-captive Plains zebra *Equus burchelli* (Schilder 1988)

Harem stallions *pushing*

131

Nip

Similar to a bite, but with the mouth less widely opened and the teeth closing on only a small piece of flesh. *Nipping* is seen during play-fighting, during mutual grooming, and during moderate to serious aggressive interactions (McDonnell and Haviland 1995).

Described in:

Horses — domestic horses and ponies (Houpt and Wolski 1980)

Przewalski horses — zoo-managed Przewalski horses (Hoffmann 1985)

Donkeys — semi-feral donkeys (S McDonnell unpublished observations)

Zebra — Cape Mountain zebra *Equus zebra zebra* (Penzhorn 1984)

Nipping during initial nose-to-nose interaction of stallion encounter

Bite Threat

Similar to bite except no contact is made. The neck is stretched and ears pinned back as the head gestures toward the target. The miss appears deliberate as opposed to accidental or successfully evaded by the target, thus giving the appearance of a warning to maintain distance. *Bite threats* are typically directed toward the target animal's head, shoulder, chest, or legs and may be performed during an aggressive forward movement such as a lunge, or toward the hind end of an opponent being chased or herded.

Other names: *bite-attempt* (Berger 1977), *mouth open and attempt to bite* (Feist 1971), *bite* (Syme and Syme 1979).

Described in:

Horses — domestic horses and ponies (Waring 1983)

Przewalski horses — zoo-managed Przewalski horses (Feh 1988, Hogan et al. 1988, Boyd and Houpt 1994)

Donkeys — feral asses *Equus asinus* (McCort 1980); feral asses *Equus africanus* (Moehlman 1974, 1998), Asiatic wild asses *Equus hemionus* (Bannikov 1971)

Zebra — semi-captive Plains zebra *Equus burchelli* (Schilder et al. 1984); Cape Mountain zebra *Equus zebra zebra* (Penzhorn 1984)

SUE MCDONNELL

Young bachelor *bite threat* to cohort

Bite

Opening and rapid closing of the jaws with the teeth grasping the flesh of another stallion. The ears are pinned and lips retracted.

Comments: Biting at each other's legs is common among bachelor stallions (Miller 1981). Berger (1986) found biting to be the primary fighting tactic of horses. Biting is also a conspicuous element of mare-stallion, stallion-mare, and mare-mare interactions.

Described in:

Horses — feral horses (Feist 1971, Welsh 1975)

Przewalski horses — zoo-managed Przewalski horses (Feh 1988, Hogan et al. 1988, Keiper 1988, Boyd and Houpt 1994)

Donkeys — Asiatic wild asses *Equus hemionus* (Bannikov 1971); feral asses *Equus africanus* (Moehlman 1974, 1998); feral asses *Equus asinus* (McCort 1980)

Zebra — Cape Mountain zebra *Equus zebra zebra* (Penzhorn 1984); semi-captive Plains zebra *Equus burchelli* (Schilder 1990)

Young bachelor *biting* cohort

Strike Threat

A strike motion that appears deliberately abbreviated or gestured so as to miss contacting the opponent. Often a part of ritualized interactions between stallions and frequently accompanied by a loud squeal or snort.

Described in:

Horses — domestic and feral horses and ponies (Waring 1983)

Przewalski horses — zoo-managed Przewalski horses (Keiper 1988, Boyd and Houpt 1994)

Zebra — Plains zebra *Equus quagga* (Klingel 1967); Cape Mountain zebra *Equus zebra zebra* (Penzhorn 1984)

Strike threat during encounter of two harem stallions on fecal pile

Strike

One or both forelegs rapidly extended forward to contact another stallion, while the hind legs remain in place. The *strike* is typically associated with arched neck threat and posturing. A stallion may also *strike* when rearing. The *strike* is often accompanied by a squeal or snort.

Other names: *front-leg kick* (Berger 1977, 1986), *paw-kick* (Feist 1971).

Comments: The *strike* also can be observed during ritualized interactions, with the usual point of impact being the ground.

Described in:

Horses — domestic and feral horses and ponies (Waring 1983)

Przewalski horses — zoo-managed Przewalski horses (Keiper 1988, Boyd and Houpt 1994)

Zebra — Plains zebra *Equus quagga* (Klingel 1967)

Kick Threat

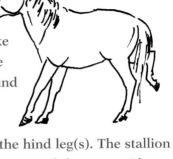

Similar to a kick, but without sufficient extension or force to make contact with the target stallion. The hind leg(s) lifts slightly off the ground and under the body in tense "readiness," usually with no subsequent backward extension of the hind leg(s). The stallion may turn his rump and may back up toward the target. The tail may lash in accompaniment and/or he may vocalize a harsh squeal. This action is often indistinguishable from the preparation for an actual kick.

Other names: *rear threat* (Wells and Von Goldschmidt-Rothschild 1979), *threat kick* (McCort 1980), *rear-leg lift* (Berger 1986), *threat to kick* (Hogan et al. 1988).

Comments: As the term *kick threat* implies, this action seems to serve as a warning, and as such, helps to maintain distance between stallions. Keiper (1988) reported that within Przewalski horse groups, the *kick threat* is second only to *herding* in frequency of aggressive actions exhibited.

Described in:

Horses — domestic and feral horses and ponies (McCort 1980, Waring 1983, Berger 1986)

Przewalski horses — zoo-managed Przewalski horses (Feh 1988, Keiper 1988, Boyd and Houpt 1994)

Donkeys — Asiatic wild asses *Equus hemionus* (Bannikov 1971); feral asses *Equus africanus* (Moehlman 1974, 1998); feral asses *Equus asinus* (McCort 1980)

Zebra — Cape Mountain zebra *Equus zebra zebra* (Penzhorn 1984); semi-captive Plains zebra *Equus burchelli* (Schilder 1990)

Kick

One or both hind legs lift off the ground and rapidly extend backward toward another stallion, with apparent intent to make contact (in contrast to the *kick threat* described on page 137). The forelegs support the weight of the body and the neck is often lowered. It is common for two stallions to simultaneously kick at each other's hindquarters, often associated with pushing each other's hindquarters.

Other names: *lift kick* (asses, McCort 1980), *hind-leg kick* (Miller 1981), *rear-leg kick* (Berger 1986), and *back kick* (Keiper 1988).

Described in:

Horses — feral horses (Berger 1986)

Przewalski horses — zoo-managed Przewalski horses (Feh 1988, Hogan et al. 1988, Boyd and Houpt 1994)

Donkeys — Asiatic wild asses *Equus hemionus* (Bannikov 1971); feral asses *Equus africanus* (Moehlman 1974, 1998); feral asses *Equus asinus* (McCort 1980)

Zebra — semi-captive Plains zebra *Equus burchelli* (Schilder 1990)

Bachelor stallion *kicking* cohort

Bachelor stallion *kicking* intruder

Bachelor and harem stallion chase with *bite threat* (left) followed by *kick* and *balk* (right)

Kneeling

Dropping to one or both knees, by one or both combatants in a close fight, or circling with mutual biting or nipping repeatedly at the knees (front and back), head, and shoulders.

Other names: *leg drop* (Berger 1986).

Comments: Berger (1986) proposed that the initial drop to the knees is an attempt to protect the forelegs from bites by the opponent. As such, this behavior may be a very important defensive action of equids.

Described in:

Horses — feral horses (Berger 1986)

Przewalski horses — zoo-confined Przewalski horses (S McDonnell unpublished observations)

Donkeys — Asiatic wild asses *Equus hemionus* (Bannikov 1971)

Zebra — semi-wild Plains zebra *Equus burchelli* (MBH Schilder personal communication 1991)

Bachelors *kneeling*

**Bachelor play-fighting
sequence initiated by a *bite
threat* (1) and *nip* (2)**

**then immediately progressing
to *grasp on leg* (3)**

and *kneeling* (4 and 5)

ELKANAH GROGAN

141

Neck Wrestle

Sparring with the head and neck. One or both partners may remain standing, drop to one or both knees, or raise the forelegs during a bout.

Other names: *neck fencing* (Berger 1986); *wrestle* (Hoffmann 1985).

Described in:

Horses — semi-feral and feral horses and ponies (Feist 1971, Tyler 1972, Blakeslee 1974, Keiper 1985, Berger 1986)

Donkeys — feral asses *Equus africanus* (Moehlman 1974, 1998)

Zebra — Cape Mountain zebra *Equus zebra zebra* (Penzhorn 1984)

Bachelor stallion sparring sequence including *follow*

rear

kneel and *neck wrestle* (3, 4, & 5)

bump and *kick threat*

Circling

Two stallions close beside one another head-to-tail, pivoting in circles, usually biting at each other's flanks, scrotum, rump, and/or hind legs. With prolonged circling, the stallions may progress lower to the ground until they reach a kneeling position or sternal recumbency, where they typically continue to bite or nip one another.

Other names: *head and neck wrestling* (Houpt and Wolski 1982), *leg drop* (Berger 1986)

Described in:

Horses — domestic and feral horses and ponies (Tembrock 1968, Waring 1983)

Przewalski horses — zoo-confined Przewalski horses (S McDonnell unpublished observations)

Donkeys — feral asses *Equus africanus* (Moehlman 1974, 1998); feral asses *Equus asinus* (McCort 1980)

Bachelors *circling*

SUE MCDONNELL

**Bachelor sparring sequence
in water, with *circling***

ELKANAH GROGAN

145

Rear

Raising of the forelegs into the air, supporting the body on the hind legs only, resulting in a near-vertical position (see also *boxing, dancing*). Two stallions will rear in close proximity and while vertical attempt to bite one another on the head and neck or strike with the forelegs. The forelegs are typically flexed at the knee and fetlock in a more or less tucked position.

Comments: *Rearing* of one or both stallions during sparring often appears to be a means of demonstrating superior height.

Described in:

Horses — feral horses (Berger 1986)

Przewalski horses — zoo-managed Przewalski horses (Boyd and Houpt 1994)

Donkeys — feral asses *Equus africanus* (Moehlman 1974, 1998); feral asses *Equus asinus* (McCort 1980)

Zebra — Cape Mountain *Equus zebra zebra* (Penzhorn 1984)

Bachelor (at center) *rearing*

Dancing

Two stallions rearing and interlocking the forelegs and shuffling the hind legs, while biting or threatening to bite one another's neck and head.

Comments: Occurs usually amidst aggressive encounters.

Described in:

Horses — domestic horses and ponies (Tembrock 1968, Waring 1983)

Przewalski horses — zoo-confined Przewalski horses (S McDonnell unpublished observations)

Donkeys — feral asses *Equus asinus* (McCort 1980)

Zebra — Cape Mountain zebra *Equus zebra zebra* (Penzhorn 1984)

Bachelor stallions *dancing*

Boxing

Two stallions in close proximity simultaneously rearing and striking out toward one another with alternate forelegs.

Comments: Occurs usually amidst aggressive encounters and may precede *dancing*.

Described in:

Horses — domestic horses and ponies (Waring 1983)

Przewalski horses — zoo-confined Przewalski horses (S McDonnell unpublished observations)

Donkeys — semi-feral donkeys (J Beach unpublished observations)

Zebra — Cape Mountain zebra *Equus zebra zebra* (Penzhorn 1984)

Bachelor stallions *boxing*

ELKANAH GROGAN

JEN PLEBANI

Harem stallions *kneeling, pushing,*
boxing, **and** *lunging*

Chase

Pursuit of another stallion, usually at a gallop in an apparent attempt to overtake, direct the movement of, or catch up with the pursued stallion. The pursuing stallion typically pins the ears, exposes the teeth, and bites at the pursued stallion's rump and tail. The stallion being chased may kick out defensively with both hind legs. *Chasing* is usually a part of fight sequences.

Described in:

Horses — domestic and feral horses and ponies (Feist 1971, Welsh 1975, Waring 1983, Berger 1986)

Przewalski horses — zoo-managed Przewalski horses (Hogan et al. 1988, Keiper 1988, Boyd and Houpt 1994)

Donkeys — feral asses *Equus africanus* (Moehlman 1974, 1998); feral asses *Equus asinus* (McCort 1980)

Zebra — semi-captive Plains zebra *Equus burchelli* (Schilder 1988, 1990)

Bachelor *chasing* cohort

Herding

Combination of head threat and ears laid back with forward locomotion, apparently directing the movement of another stallion(s).

Other names: *driving* (Wells and Von Goldschmidt-Rothschild 1979), *herding threat* (Schilder et al. 1984), *pointing* (Schilder et al. 1984), *herding posture* (Berger 1986). If the stallion's neck simultaneously oscillates from side to side, the behavior is termed *snaking* (Waring 1983).

Comments: Feist (1971) reported that *herding* is a behavior that is performed only by stallions. Although it is most common to see males herding females, male-male herding does occur.

Described in:

Horses — domestic and feral horses and ponies (Feist 1971, Welsh 1975, Miller 1981, Waring 1983)

Przewalski horses — zoo-managed Przewalski horses (Keiper 1988, Boyd and Houpt 1994)

Zebra — Cape Mountain zebra *Equus zebra zebra* (Penzhorn 1984)

SUE MCDONNELL

Harem stallion *approaching* and then *herding* intruding bachelors

Grasp

Similar to a bite, but the hold is maintained with the jaws and teeth, usually on the crest of the neck or on a foreleg above the knee or hind leg above the hock.

Other names: *biting the back of the neck* (McCort 1980).

Comments: Reportedly not common during intense fighting, but more common in play-fighting (Waring 1983). Feral asses will grasp opponents and hold them as long as possible, sometimes rearing while holding onto an ear (McCort 1980).

Described in:

Horses — feral horses (Berger 1986)

Przewalski horses — zoo-managed Przewalski horses (KA Houpt videotaped observations)

Donkeys — feral asses *Equus asinus* (McCort 1980)

Zebra — semi-wild Plains zebra *Equus burchelli* (MBH Schilder personal communication 1991)

Grasp

SUE MCDONNELL

Bachelor *grasping* foreleg of bachelor cohort

ELKANAH GROGAN

***Grasping* hind leg during encounter of three harem stallions**

Interference

Disruption of stallions' combat by moving between the combatants, by pushing, attacking, or simple approaching. One or more stallions may simultaneously interfere with an encounter.

Other names: *intervene* (asses, Bannikov 1971), *lateral presentation* (zebra, Penzhorn 1984), *interposing* (zebra, Schilder 1990).

Comments: Bannikov (1971) reported that one or more wild ass stallions will intervene to protect a weaker individual from a stronger attacker.

Described in:

Horses — feral ponies (Keiper 1988)

Donkeys — Asiatic wild asses *Equus hemionus* (Bannikov 1971)

Zebra — semi-wild Plains zebra *Equus burchelli* (Schilder 1990)

Bachelor (right) *interfering* in sparring encounter of two bachelor cohorts (left)

Rump Presentation

One stallion positions his rump squarely in front of another stallion's head, lifting the tail slightly, reminiscent of estrous presentation of mares. The stallion to whom the rump is presented usually sniffs the perineal region, and he may push his shoulder against the hindquarters, and/or rest his chin or head on the rump, and he may mount.

Comments: *Rump presentation* was exhibited by younger, lower-ranking stallions to a clearly dominant stallion.

Described in:

Horses — semi-feral ponies (McDonnell and Haviland 1995)

Erection

Extended, tumescent penis. Observed during mild to moderately intense aggressive encounters. Bachelors will mount one another with an erection, and anal insertion has been observed (S McDonnell unpublished observations).

Described in:

Horses — feral and domestic horses and ponies (Waring 1983)

Przewalski horses — zoo-confined Przewalski horses (S McDonnell unpublished observations)

Donkeys — Asiatic wild asses *Equus hemionus* (Bannikov 1971); feral asses *Equus africanus* (Moehlman 1974, 1998); feral asses *Equus asinus* (McCort 1980)

Zebra — semi-captive Plains zebra *Equus burchelli* (MBH Schilder personal communication 1991)

JEN PLEBANI

Bachelor with *erection* while sparring

Mount

One stallion raises his chest and forelegs onto the other's back with the forelegs on either side, just as during copulation. Also seen are prolonged partial mounts, typically with lateral rather than rear orientation, and often with just one foreleg across the body of the mounted stallion. In a behavior similar to the initial mount orientation movements, termed *head on neck*, *back* or *rump*, the forelegs will not actually rise off the ground. These two behaviors may occur sequentially or independently of one another.

Comments: Schilder and Boer (1987) reported *mounting* and *head-on-hindquarters* as common in the Plains zebra and suggested that this may play a role in establishing or confirming dominance hierarchies since the behaviors typically supervene fighting episodes. However, others have suggested that *mounting* represents play behavior.

Described in:

Horses — feral horses (Feist 1971, Berger 1986)

Przewalski horses — zoo-confined Przewalski horses (S McDonnell unpublished observations)

Donkeys — feral asses *Equus africanus* (Moehlman 1974, 1998)

Zebra — semi-captive Plains zebra *Equus burchelli* (Schilder 1988)

Mount with *erection* in bachelor stallion sparring session

Fecal Pile Display

A behavioral sequence occurring in association with defecation and fecal piles. Two or more stallions may participate, either simultaneously or in succession. These interactive sequences typically terminate with fighting, one stallion pushing the other away, or with calm separation as both stallions walk away from the pile.

1. Approach fecal pile
2. Sniff pile
3. Flehmen
4. Paw pile
5. Step forward over pile or pivot around pile
6. Defecate on top of pile
7. Step backward or pivot over to sniff pile
8. May repeat all or part of sequence

Other names: *elimination marking sequence* (Turner et al. 1981).

Comments: There appears to be a communication or competition aspect in this activity. It has been suggested that the last to defecate is usually the dominant stallion (McCort 1984). Miller (1981) reported that 25% of all agonistic stallion-stallion interactions took place at fecal piles.

Described in:

Horses — domestic and feral horses and ponies (Feist 1971, Welsh 1975, Waring 1983, McCort 1984, Keiper 1985)

Przewalski horses — zoo-managed Przewalski horses (Hoffmann 1985, Boyd 1988)

Donkeys — feral asses *Equus africanus* (Moehlman 1974, 1998); feral asses *Equus asinus* (McCort 1984)

Zebra — Cape Mountain zebra *Equus zebra zebra* (Penzhorn 1984)

Pawing

One foreleg is lifted from the ground slightly, then extended quickly in a forward direction, followed by movement backward dragging the toe against the ground in a digging motion. Most commonly, this action is repeated several times in succession. The stallion's nose may be oriented toward the substrate at which he is pawing or, if the activity is exhibited as a direct apparent threat to another stallion, the head will remain elevated and the neck arched. *Pawing* is frequently seen in aggressive encounters. It is also seen near fecal piles or dusty rolling sites, either as a solitary activity or during pair or group interactive encounters.

Comments: Houpt and Wolski (1982) suggested that *pawing* is a sign of frustration rather than aggression.

Described in:

Horses — domestic and feral horses (Feist 1971, Odberg 1973, Waring 1983)

Przewalski horses — zoo-managed Przewalski horses (Hoffmann 1985)

Donkeys — semi-feral donkeys (S McDonnell unpublished observations)

Pawing

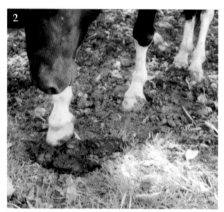

Harem stallion *sniffing feces* **(1),** *pawing* **(2), and** *urinating* **(3) over recently voided feces of mare**

Sniff Feces

Sniffing voided feces or a fecal pile, usually as a part of a *fecal pile display*. This is almost always followed by defecating over the feces and again sniffing the pile.

Other names: *elimination marking* (Turner et al. 1981).

Comments: Ewer (1968) suggested that this behavior serves to provide olfactory information about dominance ranks of stallions.

Described in:

Horses — domestic and feral horses and ponies (Welsh 1975, Berger 1977, Salter and Hudson 1982, Waring 1983)

Przewalski horses — zoo-managed Przewalski horses (Hoffmann 1985)

Donkeys — feral asses *Equus asinus* (McCort 1980)

Bachelor stallions *sniffing feces* **at stud pile**

161

Defecate Over

Defecation on fecal piles in a characteristic sequence: sniff feces, step forward, defecate, pivot or back up, and sniff feces again (see *fecal pile display*, page 158, *and sniff feces*, page 161).

Other names: *elimination marking* (Turner et al. 1981).

Comments: Stallions appear to compete to be last to defecate on a pile (McCort 1984). Order of stallions within a group to defecate may be consistent with dominance hierarchy (Feist 1971).

Described in:

Horses — feral horses (Feist 1971, Miller 1981)

Przewalski horses — zoo-confined Przewalski horses (S McDonnell unpublished observations)

Donkeys — feral asses *Equus africanus* (Moehlman 1974, 1998); feral asses *Equus asinus* (McCort 1980)

Zebra — Cape Mountain zebra *Equus zebra zebra* (Penzhorn 1984); semi-captive Plains zebra *Equus burchelli* (Schilder 1988)

Assistant harem stallion *defecates over* **feces during** *fecal pile display* **with rival harem stallion**

Two bachelors, one after the other, *sniffing*, **stepping forward, and** *defecating over* **voided urine of filly**

ELKANAH GROGAN

163

Flehmen

Head elevated and neck extended, with the eyes rolled back, the ears rotated to the side, and the upper lip everted exposing the upper incisors and adjacent gums while drawing air and fluids through the teeth. The head may roll to one side or from side to side. Typically occurs in association with *olfactory investigation* of urine or feces.

Comments: *Flehmen* is believed to facilitate the drawing of fluids into the vomeronasal organ, an accessory olfactory system with direct neural connections to the areas of the brain controlling reproductive function.

Described in:

All equids — (Schneider 1930, Stahlbaum and Houpt 1989)

Horses — feral and domestic horses and ponies (Feist 1971, Tyler 1972, Waring 1983, Keiper 1985)

Przewalski horses — zoo-managed Przewalski horses (Boyd and Houpt 1994)

Donkeys — feral asses *Equus africanus* (Moehlman 1974, 1998); feral asses *Equus asinus* (McCort 1980)

Zebra — Cape Mountain zebra *Equus zebra zebra* (Penzhorn 1984)

Flehmen **in bachelor stallion**

Examples of Extended Interaction

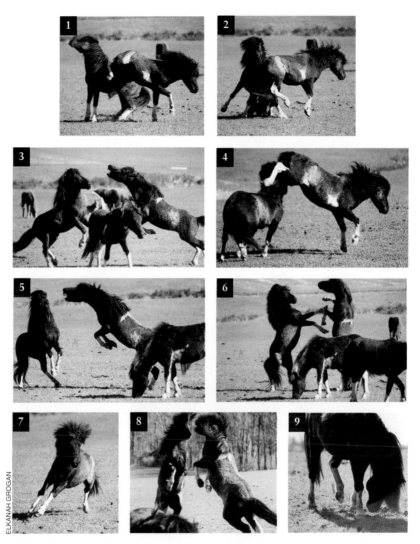

ELKANAH GROGAN

Typical extended interaction of harem stallions, including *kick, balk, rear, lunge, bite threat, dance, chase,* and *elimination marking*

Ritualized Interactive Sequence

Relatively consistently ordered agonistic sequence, described by Waring (1983):
1. *Stand stare* (*alert*)
2. *Posturing* (*arched neck threat*)
3. *Olfactory investigation*
4. *Strike threats*, *pushing*, *squealing*, and *snorting*
5. *Fecal pile displays*
6. Repetition of previous elements, often with increasing intensity

Described in:
Horses — domestic and feral horses and ponies (Welsh 1975, Waring 1983, McCort 1984)

Bachelor stallion performing
fecal pile display

Simultaneous parallel *approach*

Parallel prance

ELKANAH GROGAN

Arched neck threat **and** *bite chest*

Typical Quiet Interaction of Bachelors

Bachelors basking peacefully

Typical bachelor companion quiet interaction

Bachelor companions resting. As this resting bout progressed, the stallions alternately slept and served as sentinel

REPRODUCTIVE BEHAVIOR

HAREM FORMATION AND MAINTENANCE

BREEDING

PARTURITION, PARENTING, AND
EARLY DEVELOPMENT

HAREM FORMATION AND MAINTENANCE

The majority of a harem stallion's time is spent keeping the harem together and away from other stallions, as well as engaging in elimination marking behavior that is believed to serve a function in maintaining the harem.

Two harem stallions in battle

Tending a Harem

Continuous maintenance of proximity and attention by the harem stallion to location and activities of mares and young. Harem stallion is usually positioned as "point guard" between main herd and maximum potential threat.

Described in:

Horses — feral horses (Feist 1971, Feist and McCullough 1976, Keiper 1985)

Przewalski horses — zoo-managed Przewalski horses (Boyd and Houpt 1994)

Zebra — Cape Mountain zebra *Equus zebra zebra* (Penzhorn 1984)

Young harem stallion (rear) *tending* **his new small harem**

Alert, Approach, and Threatening Off or Attacking Intruders

Alert to Intruder

Threatening Off Intruder

SUE MCDONNELL

Harem stallion responds to intruding human male: *alert* **to intruder (1),**
approach **harem (2), and** *drive* **away harem from intruder (3)**

Herding and Driving

Basic Herding Posture

Retrieving Individual Mare

Gently Following and Directing Group Trek Led by Mature Mare

*Herding Mares Off to One Side While Addressing Potential Threat,
Such as a Passing Harem or Bachelor Group*

Herding and Driving

Moving forward with head lowered and ears back, directing the movement of one or more harem group's members.

Other names: *herding posture* (Berger 1986), *herding threat* (Schilder et al. 1984), *pointing* (Schilder et al. 1984), *driving* (Wells and Von Goldschmidt-Rothschild 1979). If the stallion's neck simultaneously oscillates from side to side, as is typical, the behavior has been called *snaking* (Waring 1983).

Comments: Feist (1971) reported that *herding* is a behavior that is performed only by stallions. While this behavior is seen mostly to keep the herd together, it is sometimes also seen to repel young visiting playmates back toward their family band.

Described in:

Horses — feral horses and ponies (Feist 1971, Welsh 1975, Feist and McCullough 1976, Miller 1981, Salter and Hudson 1982, Waring 1983, Keiper 1985)

Przewalski horses — zoo-managed Przewalski horses (Keiper 1988, Boyd and Houpt 1994)

Zebra — Cape Mountain zebra *Equus zebra zebra* (Penzhorn 1984)

Harem stallion gently *driving* a mare and foal

Elimination Marking Sequence

Sniff Feces

Flehmen Response to Feces

Defecate on Feces

Sniff Urine, Marking Location with Foreleg

Flehmen to Urine

Urinate on Urine

Defecate on Urine and Feces

Sniff Urine and Feces

Highly stylized olfactory attention of a harem stallion to recently voided urine and feces of harem members, including covering with urine and feces.

Comments: Not shown is occasional pawing of the feces before sniffing.

Described in:

Horses — feral horses and ponies (Feist 1971, Tyler 1972, Feist and McCullough 1976, Miller 1981, Turner et al. 1981, Salter and Hudson 1982, Keiper 1985)

Przewalski horses — zoo-managed Przewalski horses (Boyd and Kasman 1986)

Donkeys — feral asses *Equus africanus* (Moehlman 1974, 1998); feral asses *Equus asinus* (McCort 1980, 1984); wild asses *Equus africanus* and *Equus hemionus* (Klingel 1998)

Zebra — Cape Mountain zebra *Equus zebra zebra* (Klingel 1975, Penzhorn 1984); Plains zebra *Equus burchelli* (Klingel 1975); semi-wild Plains zebra *Equus burchelli* (Schilder 1988); Grevy's zebra *Equus grevyi* (Klingel 1975)

SUE MCDONNELL

Harem stallion *elimination marking* in response to *urination* of harem mare

Elimination Marking Sequence

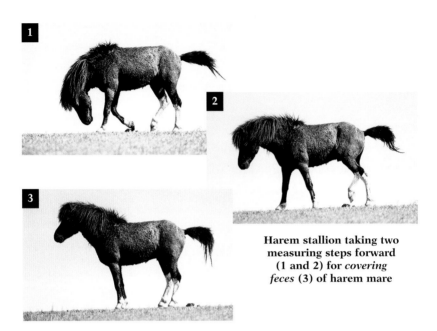

Harem stallion taking two
measuring steps forward
(1 and 2) for *covering
feces* (3) of harem mare

Harem stallion *sniffing*
and *urine-covering*
freshly voided feces
of mare

ELKANAH GROGAN

BREEDING

For harem breeders such as the horse, the harem stallion is in close contact with his mares year-round. When a mare is in estrus, the harem stallion stays near, paying increased attention to her frequent urination. Estrus includes increased activity, frequently approaching the stallion, swinging of the hindquarters toward the stallion, lifting the tail, and frequent urinations. The mare has a characteristic behavior involving rhythmic eversion of the vulva, exposing the clitoris and lighter-colored internal membranes. This is called "winking" or "flashing." The mare approaches the stallion frequently, signaling her readiness to breed. The female mating stance includes a "sawhorse squat," with the tail lifted off to the side of the perineum, the head turned back toward the stallion, and one foreleg flexed. This posture appears to assure the stallion that she will not resist being mounted. Most matings occur within less than a minute and are a relatively quiet event. Mares in estrus are typically covered by their stallion many times per day, with intervals between breedings as short as a few minutes.

In addition to mature harem mares, young mares that are either still in their natal band, or in transitional gangs of young males and females, typically solicit and are bred by many different young and bachelor stallions. These young mares, when in estrus, tend to wander from their natal or transitional band, seeking and tolerating breeding from many different stallions and often from gangs of young males that breed the filly in orderly rapid succession.

Precopulatory Sequence
Tending Estrous Mares

Tending Individual Mare Near Estrus

Maintaining close proximity during ongoing feeding and resting activities, often with synchrony of movement that suggests vigilant mutual attentiveness.

Comments: While harem stallions appear attentive to their herd members more or less all the time, this tending of mares in estrus clearly represents a heightened attentiveness.

Described in:

Horses — feral and semi-feral horses and ponies (Feist 1971, Waring 1983, Keiper 1985)

Przewalski horses — zoo-confined Przewalski horses (S McDonnell unpublished observations)

Zebra — Cape Mountain zebra *Equus zebra zebra* (Penzhorn 1984)

Distant Approach

Approaching a female from a distance, usually vocalizing with a long, loud whinny. Most commonly seen in a bachelor to an approaching young mare, or occasionally in a harem stallion upon returning to his harem after expelling an intruder to some distance away from the harem mares.

Comments: Disturbances of the herd tend to stimulate sexual activity. So upon returning from expelling an intruder or bachelor challenger, if there is a mare in estrus, teasing and breeding almost always occur.

Described in:

Horses — feral and semi-feral horses and ponies (Feist 1971, Waring 1983, Keiper 1985)

Przewalski horses — zoo-confined Przewalski horses (S McDonnell unpublished observations)

Donkeys — feral asses *Equus africanus* (Moehlman 1974, 1998)

Zebra — captive-bred Grevy's zebra *Equus grevyi* and Grant's zebra *Equus burchelli boehmi* (McDonnell unpublished observations)

Head-to-Head Approach

Stallion and mare facing one another as they come into close proximity for precopulatory or copulatory interaction.

Described in:

Horses — feral and semi-feral horses and ponies (Feist 1971, Waring 1983, Keiper 1985)

Przewalski horses — zoo-confined Przewalski horses (S McDonnell unpublished observations)

Donkeys — semi-feral donkeys (Henry et al. 1991)

Zebra — Cape Mountain zebra *Equus zebra zebra* (Penzhorn 1984)

**Harem mare and stallion approaching *head-to-head* during precopulatory
interaction (Note that their interested yearling is tolerated.)**

Head-to-Rear Approach (Receptive Mare)

Stallion and mare initiate precopulatory interaction by the stallion approaching the mare from the rear. Mare typically turns head to face stallion as he approaches.

Described in:

Horses — feral and semi-feral horses and ponies (Feist 1971, Waring 1983, Keiper 1985)

Przewalski horses — zoo-confined Przewalski horses (S McDonnell unpublished observations)

Donkeys — feral asses *Equus asinus* (McCort 1980); semi-feral donkeys (Henry et al. 1991)

Zebra — Cape Mountain zebra *Equus zebra zebra* (Penzhorn 1984)

ELKANAH GROGAN

Head-to-rear approach during
precopulatory interaction of a
harem stallion and mare,
illustrating alternating solicitation
(1,2,3, & 4) and non-receptive
behavior of mare (5)

Teasing Sequence

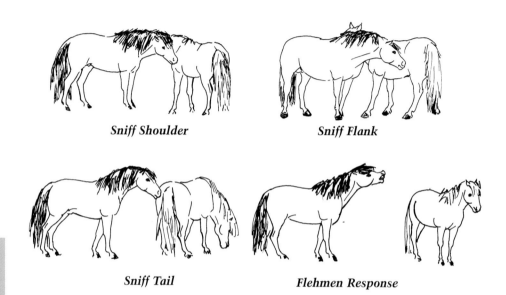

Sniff Shoulder   **Sniff Flank**

Sniff Tail   **Flehmen Response**

Precopulatory investigation of the female by the male and
sometimes of the male by the female.

Described in:

Horses — feral and semi-feral horses and ponies (Feist 1971,
Waring 1983, Keiper 1985)

Przewalski horses — zoo-managed Przewalski horses (Houpt and
Boyd 1994)

Donkeys — feral asses *Equus asinus* (McCort 1980, 1984); semi-
feral donkeys (Henry et al. 1991)

Zebra — Cape Mountain zebra *Equus zebra zebra* (Penzhorn 1984)

Penis Drop

Relaxation and protrusion of the penis from the prepuce.

Described in:

Horses — feral and semi-feral horses and ponies (Feist 1971, Waring 1983, Keiper 1985)

Przewalski horses — zoo-confined Przewalski horses (S McDonnell unpublished observations)

Donkeys — semi-feral donkeys (Henry et al. 1991)

Zebra — Cape Mountain zebra *Equus zebra zebra* (Penzhorn 1984)

Penis drop during teasing

Chin Rest and Chest Bump

During precopulatory interaction, often immediately before mounting, the stallion stands behind the mare with his chest against the hindquarters and his chin resting or pressing along the dorsal midline of the mare.

Described in:

Horses — feral and semi-feral horses and ponies (Feist 1971, Waring 1983, Keiper 1985)

Przewalski horses — zoo-managed Przewalski horses (Houpt and Boyd 1994)

Donkeys — feral asses *Equus asinus* (McCort 1980); semi-feral donkeys (Henry et al. 1991)

Zebra — Cape Mountain zebra *Equus zebra zebra* (Penzhorn 1984)

Chin rest and *chest bump* during precopulatory interaction
of harem mare and stallion

Mount Without Erection

Without a penile erection, a stallion raises his forelegs
and fore body to rest the ventral abdomen and chest upon
the hindquarters of the mare, grasping around the body of
the mare with the forelegs and sometimes grasping onto
the mane and crest of the mare's neck with the teeth.

Described in:

Horses — feral and semi-feral horses and ponies (Waring 1983,
Keiper 1985)

Przewalski horses — zoo-confined Przewalski horses (S McDonnell
unpublished observations)

Donkeys — feral asses *Equus asinus* (McCort 1980); semi-feral
donkeys (Henry et al. 1991); wild asses *Equus africanus* and
Equus hemionus (Klingel 1998)

Zebra — Cape Mountain zebra *Equus zebra zebra* (Penzhorn 1984)

Lean

During precopulatory interaction, a stallion and mare push against one another. Typically the stallion pushes with his chest and shoulder and the mare with her shoulder and flank.

Comments: As with *chin rest* and *chin bump,* the lean appears to be a "testing" of the mare's readiness to tolerate being mounted.

Described in:

Horses — feral and semi-feral horses and ponies (Feist 1971)

Przewalski horses — zoo-managed Przewalski horses (Houpt and Boyd 1994)

Donkeys — feral asses *Equus asinus* (McCort 1980); semi-feral donkeys (Henry et al. 1991)

Zebra — Cape Mountain zebra *Equus zebra zebra* (Penzhorn 1984)

Lateral Mount

A stallion's lifting of his forelegs and fore body upon the mare with his legs and chest across the long axis of her back.

Described in:

Horses — feral horses (Feist 1971, Keiper 1985)

Przewalski horses — zoo-confined Przewalski horses (S McDonnell unpublished observations)

Donkeys — feral asses *Equus asinus* (McCort 1980); semi-feral donkeys (Henry et al. 1991)

Roll Near Mare

A stallion's rolling sequence when tending a mare in
estrus, either before or after precopulatory and copulatory
interaction. Elimination marking behavior may
accompany the rolling sequence.

Described in:

Horses — semi-feral ponies and domestic pasture-bred horses
(S McDonnell unpublished observations)

Przewalski horses — zoo-confined Przewalski horses (S McDonnell
unpublished observations)

Donkeys — semi-feral donkeys (Henry et al. 1991)

**Harem stallion *rolling* near harem
mare in estrus (at left)**

AMY POULIN

Non-Receptive Female Responses

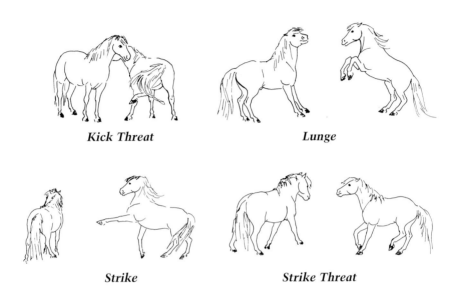

Kick Threat   *Lunge*

Strike   *Strike Threat*

Any of a number of mildly to strongly aggressive threats or avoidance behaviors displayed by mares to precopulatory interactions of a stallion.

Comments: Horse mares typically go through several days of estrus before reliably standing for breeding, during which they may alternately solicit and rebuff a stallion.

Described in:

Horses — feral and semi-feral horses and ponies (Feist 1971, Waring 1983, Keiper 1985)

Przewalski horses — zoo-confined Przewalski horses (S McDonnell unpublished observations)

Donkeys — feral asses *Equus africanus* (Moehlman 1974, 1998); feral asses *Equus asinus* (McCort 1980); semi-feral donkeys (Henry et al. 1991); wild asses *Equus africanus* and *Equus hemionus* (Klingel 1998)

Zebra — Cape Mountain zebra *Equus zebra zebra* (Penzhorn 1984)

Non-Receptive Female Responses

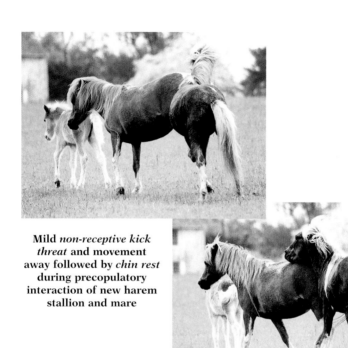

Mild *non-receptive kick threat* and movement away followed by *chin rest* during precopulatory interaction of new harem stallion and mare

ELKANAH GROGAN

Moderately *non-receptive kick threat* during precopulatory interaction of harem stallion and mare

Receptive Female Responses

Backing into Stallion

***Mare Winking and
"Breaking Down"***

***Saw Horse Stance with
Head Turned Back***

Stand for Mounting

Mare *winking* vulva

Copulatory Sequence
Mount with Erection and Insertion

Standing squarely behind or with the fore body slightly to one side of the mare, the stallion lifts his forelegs and fore body to rest his ventral abdomen and chest upon the back of the mare, grasps around the body of the mare with the forelegs and sometimes grasps onto the mane and crest of the mare's neck with the teeth.

Described in:

Horses — feral and semi-feral horses and ponies (Feist 1971, Waring 1983, Keiper 1985)

Przewalski horses — zoo-managed Przewalski horses (Houpt and Boyd 1994)

Donkeys — feral asses *Equus africanus* (Moehlman 1974, 1998); feral asses *Equus asinus* (McCort 1980); semi-feral donkeys (Henry et al. 1991); wild asses *Equus africanus* and *Equus hemionus* (Klingel 1998)

Zebra — Cape Mountain zebra *Equus zebra zebra* (Penzhorn 1984)

Ejaculation

Following thrusting (usually 7 to 9 well-organized, rhythmic pelvic thrusts), the emission and expulsion of semen (typically 7 to 12 urethral pulses and corresponding jets of semen). The tail waves or "flags," corresponding to ejaculatory contractions of the urethra.

Comments: When positioning and insertion are normal, the glans penis tumesces (flowers, bells, flares) just before ejaculation, establishing a sealed contact with the cervix of the mare such that semen is deposited directly from the urethral process into the uterus.

Described in:

Horses — feral and semi-feral horses and ponies (Feist 1971, Waring 1983, Keiper 1985)

Przewalski horses — zoo-managed Przewalski horses (Houpt and Boyd 1994)

Donkeys — feral asses *Equus africanus* (Moehlman 1974, 1998); feral asses *Equus asinus* (McCort 1980); semi-feral donkeys (Henry et al. 1991); wild asses *Equus africanus* and *Equus hemionus* (Klingel 1998)

Zebra — Cape Mountain zebra *Equus zebra zebra* (Penzhorn 1984)

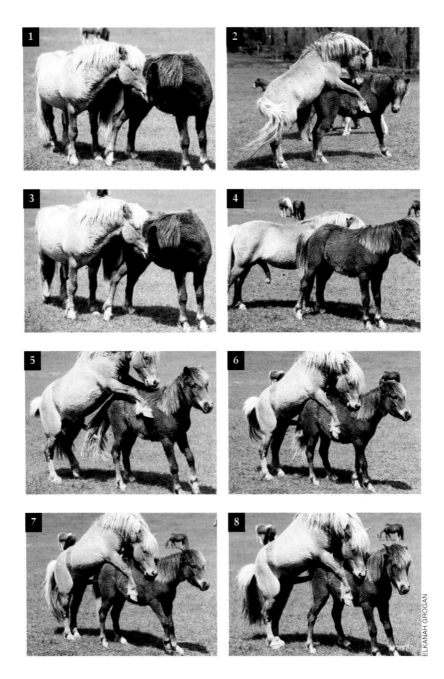

Teasing, receptive, and facilitatory behavior during a precopulatory and
copulatory interaction of a harem stallion and a wandering yearling filly
(Note filly's postural adjustments to facilitate and accommodate insertion
and her lingering with the stallion following breeding.)

Ejaculation during breeding of harem mare and stallion

PARTURITION, PARENTING, AND EARLY DEVELOPMENT

Gestation (pregnancy) lasts about 11 months in horses. There is very little change in behavior with pregnancy or until immediately before parturition (birth). Most parturition occurs in the evening or near daybreak. Some especially vigilant stallions appear to sequester their harem in a sheltered area away from other harems

Increased *alert* and patrolling by stallion as harem mare commences Stage II labor

when a mare is foaling. They patrol and mark the area. The harem may continue to keep its distance from other groups for the first days or as long as a week after parturition.

Parturition is very quick in horses, often only minutes from any sign of discomfort until the foal is born. We have witnessed several foalings in our semi-feral herd in which the time frame from the first sign of discomfort of the mare until the foal was born and standing, and ready to move with the herd if necessary, spanned only 10 to 20 minutes.

The mare initially shows signs of abdominal discomfort, getting up and down frequently. Once the fetal fluids erupt, the mare typically remains recumbent for foaling. The family members often gather around the birth event, sometimes vocalizing to the foal during parturition. The mare immediately attends the foal with licking that clears the birth membranes and appears to stimulate the foal. The mare sniffs and may perform the Flehmen response to the expelled fetal membranes. Unlike some species, mares rarely eat the placenta. The foal and dam bond quite rapidly under natural conditions. Even in harem groups with foals born on the same day, cross-nursing or behavior suggesting inadequate bonding between a mare and foal is rarely observed.

Foals are precocious. Those born under natural conditions often stand, nurse, and are ready to run with the herd within the first half-hour of life. Most maintenance behaviors are present in the foal within hours of birth, including elimination, self and mutual grooming, investigation, mouthing of vegetation, social communication including threats and overt aggression, and locomotor sequences. Explosive locomotor and play behavior is conspicuous, usually on the second day.

Both the mare and stallion are protective and tolerant of the young. For the first week or two, the foal's nearest neighbor is almost always the dam, but should any disturbance occur, the harem stallion shows strong protective behavior for the young. The mare usually plays the primary parenting role, including providing protection, for the first week or so, after which the stallion plays an increasingly active role in parenting. This includes primarily retrieving straying youngsters and occasionally playing with foals and yearlings.

Weaning occurs gradually in horses. While some yearlings stop nursing before the subsequent sibling is born, many yearlings and two-year-olds still nurse occasionally. Nursing by yearlings and older offspring may be particularly more common in populations that have good year-round nutrition, where mares likely maintain milk year-round.

SUE MCDONNELL

Bay harem stallion (left) and black-and-white assistant harem stallion (right) flanking their harem during a foaling

Parturition

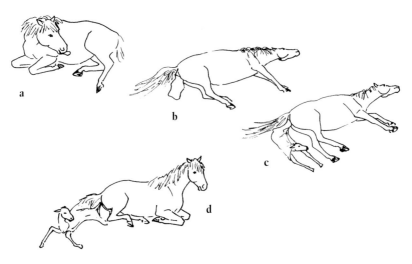

a

b

c

d

Expulsion of the foal and fetal membranes. Stage I Labor: abdominal discomfort (a). Stage II Labor: chorioallantoic membrane presentation, rupture, and release of allantoic fluid (b), expulsion of the foal (c and d). Stage III (not shown) consists of expulsion of the fetal membranes.

Other names: *foaling* (Feist 1971, Keiper 1985); *giving birth* (Boyd 1980).

Comments: Under natural herd conditions, usually little behavioral indication of imminent parturition. The umbilical cord often separates as the mare stands between Stage II and Stage III. If the mare is slow to rise it may break as the foal attempts to rise.

Described in:

Horses — feral and semi-feral horses and ponies (Tyler 1972, Blakeslee 1974, Boyd 1980, Crowell-Davis 1986)

Przewalski horses — zoo-managed Przewalski horses (Boyd 1988)

Donkeys — semi-feral donkeys (J Beach unpublished observations)

Sniff/Lick Membranes

Olfactory attention to the expelled fetal fluids and membranes.

Described in:

Horses — feral and semi-feral horses and ponies (Tyler 1972, Blakeslee 1974, Boyd 1980, Keiper 1985, Crowell-Davis 1986)

Przewalski horses — zoo-managed Przewalski horses (Boyd 1988)

Donkeys — semi-feral donkeys (J Beach unpublished observations)

Zebra — Plains zebra *Equus burchelli* (Klingel 1969); Grevy's zebra *Equus grevyi* (Gardner 1983)

Mare and stallion *sniffing* expelled fetal membranes

Flehmen Response

Head elevated and neck extended, with the eyes rolled back, the ears rotated to the side, and the upper lip everted exposing the upper incisors and adjacent gums. The head may roll to one side or from side to side.

Comments: *Flehmen* is believed to facilitate the drawing of fluids into the vomeronasal organ, enhancing the horse's olfactory capacity. Eating of the placenta is rare but instances have been noted in horses (KA Houpt personal communication) and Plains zebra (Klingel 1969)

Described in:

All equids — (Schneider 1930, Stahlbaum and Houpt 1989)

Horses — feral and domestic horses and ponies (Feist 1971, Tyler 1972, Boyd 1980)

Przewalski horses — zoo-managed Przewalski horses (Boyd and Houpt 1994)

Donkeys — feral asses *Equus africanus* (Moehlman 1974, 1998); feral asses *Equus asinus* (McCort 1980)

Zebra — Cape Mountain zebra *Equus zebra zebra* (Penzhorn 1984)

Sniff/Lick/Nuzzle Foal

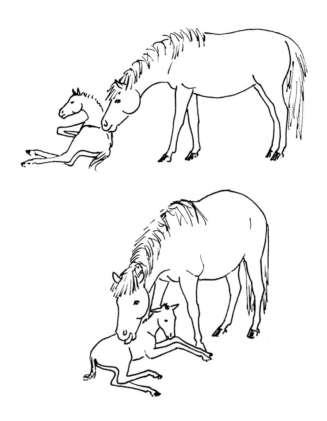

Oronasal contact of dam to neonate, presumed to clean and
stimulate the foal as well as provide bonding cues to the mare.

Described in:

Horses — feral and semi-feral horses and ponies (Tyler 1972,
Blakeslee 1974, Boyd 1980, Keiper 1985, Crowell-Davis 1986)

Przewalski horses — zoo-managed Przewalski horses (Boyd 1988)

Donkeys — semi-feral donkeys (J Beach unpublished observations)

Zebra — Plains zebra *Equus burchelli* (Klingel 1969); Grevy's
zebra *Equus grevyi* (Gardner 1983)

Foal Attempt to Stand

Attempts of neonate to rise to feet; usually includes several awkward or wobbly failed attempts.

Described in:

Horses — feral and semi-feral horses and ponies (Blakeslee 1974, Boyd 1980, Keiper 1985)

Przewalski horses — zoo-managed Przewalski horses (Boyd 1988)

Donkeys — semi-feral donkeys (J Beach unpublished observations)

Zebra — Grevy's zebra *Equus grevyi* (Gardner 1983)

Minutes-old neonate *attempting to stand*

Mare and Foal Nose-to-Nose

The mare and neonate's prolonged sniffing of one another at the nose.

Described in:

Horses — feral and semi-feral horses and ponies (Blakeslee 1974, Boyd 1980)

Przewalski horses — zoo-managed Przewalski horses (Boyd 1988)

Donkeys — semi-feral donkeys (J Beach unpublished observations)

Zebra — Grevy's zebra *Equus grevyi* (Gardner 1983)

Mare and neonate *sniffing* and *nuzzling* noses

Mare Sniff/Lick/Nuzzle Foal Perineum

Prolonged and repeated oronasal contact of the dam to the foal's anal area.

Described in:

Horses — feral and semi-feral horses and ponies (Blakeslee 1974, Boyd 1980)

Przewalski horses — zoo-managed Przewalski horses (Boyd 1988)

Donkeys — semi-feral donkeys (J Beach unpublished observations)

Zebra — Grevy's zebra *Equus grevyi* (Gardner 1983)

Mare *sniffing* and *nuzzling* perineum of neonate

Parturition Sequence

9:47 a.m. — First Behavioral Evidence of Stage I Labor

Harem stallion patrolling
perimeter of harem, *chasing*
other harems away

Harem youngsters gathering
around mare showing signs of
abdominal discomfort

Flehmen response

SUE MCDONNELL

Investigating and covering frequent
urinations of mare

Parturition Sequence

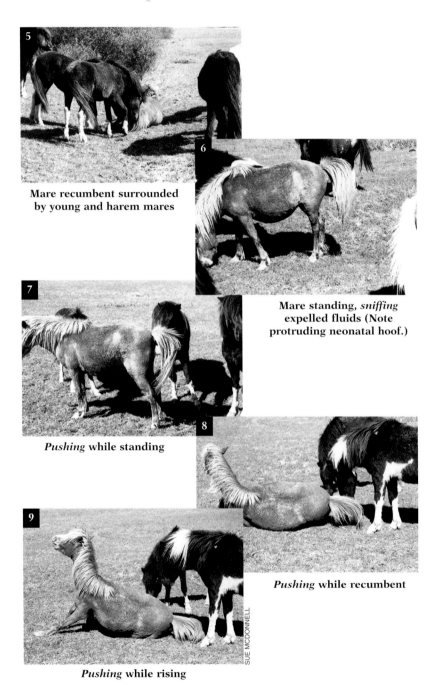

5 Mare recumbent surrounded by young and harem mares

6 Mare standing, *sniffing* expelled fluids (Note protruding neonatal hoof.)

7 *Pushing* while standing

8 *Pushing* while recumbent

9 *Pushing* while rising

SUE MCDONNELL

**Breaking fluids — Onset of
Stage II Labor**

**Mare and family
investigating fluids**

Pushing **while going down**

Strong contraction and straining

Parturition Sequence

**Momentary
recumbent rest**

Rising

Standing rest (Note harem
stallion and older male
offspring patrolling and
marking the area, keeping
other harems at an increasing
distance from birth site.)

**Mare "throwing herself" from
standing into a recumbent
push**

Intense straining

212

Standing rest

**Harem two-year-old male
nuzzling and nickering to
half-born neonate, foal
responding vocally**

9:54 a.m.

**Final push — End of Stage II
Labor**

SUE MCDONNELL

**Mare immediately rises, investigates
neonate as it lands on haunches**

213

Parturition Sequence

9:54 a.m.

9:56 a.m.

Neonate stands

Mare down, passing fetal
membranes (Stage III Labor)

Mare immediately stands,
investigates fetal membranes

Mare alert to harem stallion
and older male offspring
moving other harems away

Harem stallion approaches site,
investigates placenta

SUE MCDONNELL

214

Harem stallion investigates foal

10:01 a.m.

Dam threatens harem
youngster and harem
stallion
away from foal

SUE MCDONNELL

215

Parturition Sequence

Nose-to-nose contact of dam and neonate

Neonate seeking udder

Neonate seeking udder

Dam threatening off harem yearlings

Neonate seeking udder

Neonate approaching another harem mare

SUE MCDONNELL

Neonate approaching another harem mare

Neonate back to dam

Dam facilitating nursing

10:02 a.m.

Successful nursing

Foal starting to pass first feces

217

Parturition Sequence

Mare has cleared family members;
foal begins circling dam

Harem stallion and older offspring
sparring around the perimeter of
the birth site

10:08 a.m.

SUE MCDONNELL

Nursing

Reverse Parallel

Perpendicular

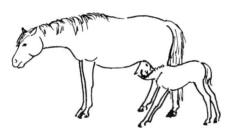

Parallel

Rear Through Hind Legs

Three Generations
(seen occasionally)

Nursing

Other names: *suckling.*

Comments: Most nursing bouts commence with the foal butting or bunting the udder with its head. This stimulates milk letdown. Foals will sometimes attempt to nurse or successfully nurse a recumbent dam. Mares typically position themselves to facilitate access to the udder. This may include widening the stance or moving the near hind leg back. Nursing and/or just udder contact and/or bunting occurs reliably upon rising after rest, immediately following resolution of a disturbance, after play bouts, and immediately upon return to the dam following separation. Cross-nursing with a mare other than the dam is uncommon and only occasionally seen in very young foals under natural conditions.

Described in:

Horses — feral and semi-feral horses and ponies (Feist 1971, Tyler 1972, Blakeslee 1974, Boyd 1980, Keiper 1985, Crowell-Davis 1986)

Przewalski horses — zoo-managed Przewalski horses (Houpt and Boyd 1994)

Donkeys — feral asses *Equus africanus* (Moehlman 1974, 1998)

Zebra — Grevy's zebra *Equus grevyi* (Gardner 1983); Cape Mountain zebra *Equus zebra zebra* (Penzhorn 1984)

Close-up views of foal *nursing*

Mare facilitating neonate's first *nursing*

Mare facilitating *nursing*; nudging and stabilizing neonate

221

Nursing

Nursing — parallel position

Nursing — perpendicular
position

Nursing — recumbent dam

Yearling *nursing*

222

Blocking

Circling around a moving mare and stopping in front of and perpendicular to the mare as foal passes under her neck. This appears to stop the mare's forward movement and elicit her facilitation of the foal's nursing.

Other names: *crossing the bows* (Joubert 1972).

Described in:

Horses — domestic horses and ponies (Tyler 1972; Blakeslee 1974; Crowell-Davis 1986)

Przewalski horses — zoo-managed Przewalski horses (Houpt and Boyd 1994)

Donkeys — feral asses *Equus asinus* (McCort 1980)

Zebra — Grevy's zebra *Equus grevyi* (Gardner 1974; Becker and Ginsberg 1990); Cape Mountain zebra *Equus zebra zebra* (Penzhorn 1984)

Blocking **in a day-old-foal**

Following

As mare moves, foal moves along at similar or faster gait, maintaining proximity that varies with age.

Comments: Foals reportedly maintain proximity of 1 meter or less for 85% and 5 meters or less for 94% to 99% of time during first week of life (Tyler 1972, Crowell-Davis 1986). While mares will sometimes follow the foal, the majority of following is done by the foal.

Described in:

Horses — feral and semi-feral horses and ponies (Feist 1971, Tyler 1972, Blakeslee 1974, Boyd 1980, Keiper 1985, Crowell-Davis 1986)

Przewalski horses — zoo-managed Przewalski horses (Boyd 1988)

Donkeys — feral asses *Equus asinus* (McCort 1980)

Zebra — Grevy's Zebra *Equus grevyi* (Gardner 1974, Becker and Ginsberg 1990); Cape Mountain zebra *Equus zebra zebra* (Penzhorn 1984)

Day-old neonate *following* **at a** *gallop*

Snapping

Moving the lower jaw up and down in a chewing or sucking motion, usually with the mouth open and lips drawn back exposing the incisors. A sucking sound may be made as the tongue is drawn against the roof of the mouth (Waring 1983). Typically, the head and neck are extended, with the ears relaxed and oriented back or laterally. It is usually performed while approaching the head of another, usually on an angle.

Other names: *Unterlegenheitsgebarde* (Zeeb 1959), *teeth-clapping* (Feist 1971), *jawing* (asses, Moehlman 1974, 1998; McCort 1980), *jaw-waving* (Blakeslee 1974), *champing* (Wolski et al. 1980), *tooth-clapping* (Boyd 1980; Przewalski horses, Feh 1988), *bared-teeth face* (zebra, Schilder and Boer 1987).

Comments: The name *snapping* was first used by Tyler (1972). It is commonly interpreted as indicating submission. Boyd (1980) concluded that *snapping* does not inhibit aggression by others but instead may serve to calm the submissive individual. Crowell-Davis (Crowell-Davis et al. 1985) suggested that snapping may be a "displacement activity developed from nursing." A similar behavior, commonly called *jawing*, occurs at estrus in asses.

Described in:

Horses — domestic and feral horses and ponies (Feist 1971, Wells and Von Goldschmidt-Rothschild 1979, Crowell-Davis 1983)

Snapping

Przewalski horses — zoo-managed Przewalski horses (Feh 1988, Hogan et al. 1988, Boyd 1988, Boyd and Houpt 1994)

Donkeys — feral asses *Equus africanus* (Moehlman 1974, 1998); feral asses *Equus asinus* (McCort 1980); semi-feral donkeys (S McDonnell unpublished data)

Zebra — semi-captive Plains zebra *Equus burchelli* (Schilder et al. 1984)

Coprophagy

Coprophagy in a
days-old foal

AMY POULIN

Coprophagy

Ingest feces by using lips and tongue to draw feces into the mouth, chew, and swallow.

Comments: Normal developmental behavior of foals beginning as early as first week and continuing for a few months, with greatest frequency during first two months (Crowell-Davis and Houpt 1985).

Described in:

Horses — domestic and feral horses and ponies (Hafez et al. 1962, Tyler 1972, Feist and McCullough 1976, Waring 1983, Crowell-Davis and Houpt 1985)

Przewalski horses — zoo-managed Przewalski horses (Boyd and Houpt 1994)

Donkeys — semi-feral donkeys (J Beach unpublished observations)

Zebra — Cape Mountain zebra *Equus zebra zebra* (Penzhorn 1984)

Young foal eating freshly voided feces of dam

Tending a Foal

Maintaining close proximity and attention to the neonatal foal, usually by the mare and/or harem stallion.

Other names: *recumbency response* (Crowell-Davis 1986).

Described in:

Horses — domestic horses and ponies (Tyler 1972, Blakeslee 1974, Boyd 1980, Crowell-Davis 1986)

Przewalski horses — zoo-managed Przewalski horses (Boyd 1988)

Donkeys — feral asses *Equus africanus* (Moehlman 1974, 1998)

Zebra — Cape Mountain zebra *Equus zebra zebra* (Penzhorn 1984); Grevy's Zebra *Equus grevyi* (Becker and Ginsberg 1990)

Note: Grevy's zebra have territorial rather than harem social organization and so do not have long-lasting affiliations among mares. In arid environments lactating mares with young foals form kindergartens of their foals. One or two mares or a stallion stays behind with the kindergarten while other dams trek to water (Klingel 1975, Becker and Ginsberg 1990).

Dam *tending*/protecting recumbent neonate

Dams and harem stallions *tending* neonates

229

Parental Protection of Foal

Guarding of the foal by either the dam or harem stallion,
threatening or driving off herd mates or intruders.

Described in:

Horses — domestic and feral horses and ponies (Feist 1971, Tyler
1972, Blakeslee 1974, Boyd 1980, Keiper 1985, Crowell-Davis
1986)

Przewalski horses — zoo-managed Przewalski horses (Boyd 1988)

Donkeys — feral asses *Equus africanus* (Moehlman 1974, 1998)

Zebra — Cape Mountain zebra *Equus zebra zebra* (Penzhorn 1984)

**Dam of neonate (foreground)
showing mild *head threat*
to curious herd mate**

ELKANAH GROGAN

Stallion with mare and minutes-old neonate at birth site

Harem adults clustering around foals during trek to water

Parental Protection of Foal

**Dam *tending* one-hour-old
neonate and expelling
curious family members**

SUE MCDONNELL

232

Parental Tolerance of Foal

Tolerate foals underfoot — investigating, playing on, bumping into adults.

Comments: Foal sexual behavior toward the dam occurs reliably for both colts and fillies when the dam is in estrus, particularly conspicuous at the first postpartum estrus at about one week. Both the dam and the harem stallion are extraordinarily tolerant of the foal's lingering at the tail of the mare, olfactory investigations, and mounting. In our semi-feral herd of ponies, we have observed stallions waiting for the foal to complete a sexual sequence before proceeding with breeding of the mare.

Described in:

Horses — feral and semi-feral horses and ponies (Boyd 1980, Keiper 1985, Berger 1986)

Przewalski horses — zoo-managed Przewalski horses (Houpt and Boyd 1994)

Donkeys — feral asses *Equus africanus* (Moehlman 1974, 1998)

Zebra — Plains zebra *Equus burchelli* (Klingel 1969); Cape Mountain zebra *Equus zebra zebra* (Penzhorn 1984)

Parental Tolerance of Foal

Mare *tolerating* foal *nipping* ear (left) and *pulling* mane (right)

Sire and dam *tolerating* yearling's sexual interaction during breeding

Dam *tolerating* foal's sexual investigation

234

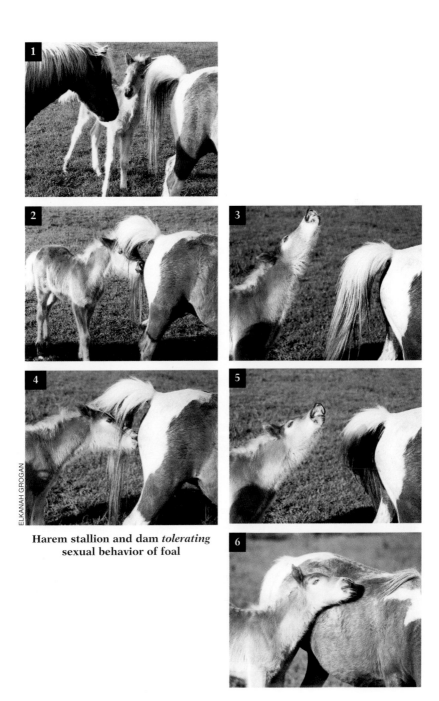

ELKANAH GROGAN

**Harem stallion and dam *tolerating*
sexual behavior of foal**

Parental Play with Young

Engaging in or a willing target of play with offspring. In horses, almost always the sire rather than the dam, and most commonly, although not exclusively a yearling and older males rather than younger foals or fillies.

Described in:

Horses — feral horses (Berger 1986)

Przewalski horses — zoo-managed Przewalski horses (Houpt and Boyd 1994)

Donkeys — semi-feral donkeys (J Beach unpublished observations)

Sire in *play* **with young foal**

Early Developmental Behavior
Photographed Examples

**20-minute-old neonate *walking* and
trotting circles around dam (1-4),
and *jumping* over the passed
placenta (5)**

SUE MCDONNELL

237

Early Developmental Behavior

Neonate passing first feces (meconium)

Early Developmental Behavior

Standing sleep and *recumbent sleep* in day-old neonates

ELKANAH GROGAN

Early Developmental Behavior

Typical *nursing* and resting sequence of day-old foal

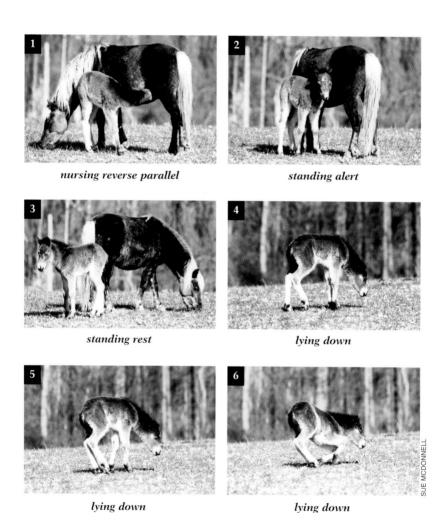

nursing reverse parallel

standing alert

standing rest

lying down

lying down

lying down

SUE MCDONNELL

Early Developmental Behavior

lying down

sternal recumbency

dam in *sternal recumbency* near foal

foal in *lateral recumbency*

SUE MCDONNELL

foal up and *stretch*

241

Early Developmental Behavior

Yawning in days-old neonate

Rolling in days-old neonate

Early Developmental Behavior

SUE MCDONNELL

Grazing attempt, *walk* under dam, *autogrooming*, and *following* in one-hour-old foal

243

Early Developmental Behavior

Grazing and *browsing*
in days-old neonate

Alert in foal

Stretching in days-old neonate

Early Developmental Behavior

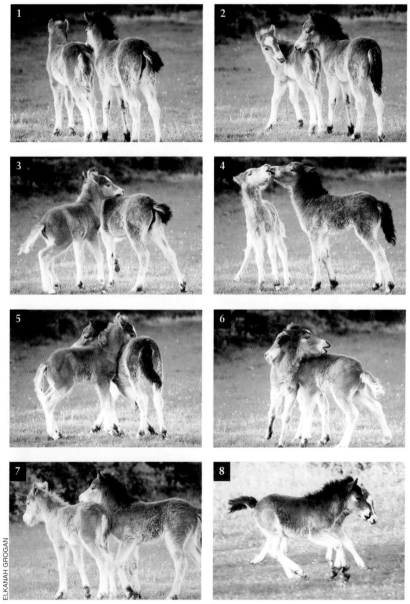

Typical interaction sequence between days-old playmates

Early Developmental Behavior

Sniffing and *licking* dam at foal heat

Spontaneous *erection* and penile movements

SECTION V

PLAY

Play behavior is a remarkably conspicuous feature of equid developmental behavior (Fagen 1977, 1981). Play has been broadly characterized as activities appearing to have no immediate use or function to the animal, involving a sense of pleasure and elements of surprise (McFarland 1987). Across species, play behavior in large part appears to be a modified form of serious survival activities such as locomotor, aggressive, and reproductive behavior. In any species, play is usually distinguished from serious forms of behavior by postures and expressions denoting less serious "intent" (Schilder et al. 1984). In most species, play behavior occurs both as a solitary activity and as a social interactive behavior. Play is believed to serve a variety of adaptive functions, including enhancing general musculoskeletal and cardiovascular fitness, practicing and honing specific survival skills, gaining familiarity with the particular environment, or building social relationships and communication skills (Fagen 1981, Bekoff and Byers 1998).

While play is most frequent and conspicuous in foals, yearlings, and bachelors, it also occurs in mature adults. Among adults it appears most common in bachelor stallions. Within harem groups it appears to be more common in the harem stallion than in mature mares.

It is sometimes unclear whether particular behaviors associated with play should be considered as elements of play or as initiators or terminators of play. For example, social play bouts often are preceded by a mutual *head toss* or *alert* posture (McDonnell and Haviland 1995). It is not clear whether these represent play or play initiation gestures. Also, when studying play behavior, it is not easy to decide whether certain behaviors have a play form or are always serious behavior in young foals. For example, some authors have considered mutual grooming, self-grooming, or rolling as play behavior in the horse (McGreevy 1996, Tyler 1972). It is difficult to judge whether these behaviors serve a serious grooming purpose as in adults or represent play forms of the behavior. In our direct observations of ponies and horses, for each of these examples the behavior has occurred in complete form and sequence with seemingly serious intent similar to that of adults. So, for example, in mutual grooming the nips among week-old foals appear as complete as those among adults. Rolling of foals has been observed in response to a novel substrate or a fresh puddle, in which case it has been interpreted as play rolling (S Ralston, personal communication).

Another example where the distinction between play and serious behavior is unclear concerns grazing or drinking behavior. Before foals begin ingesting grass or drinking water, they all appear to go through a brief developmental stage during which they seem to mimic the grazing or drinking behavior of adults in a playful investigative manner, mouthing and chewing but not ingesting (Blakeslee 1974). In our observations of pony and horse foals, this phase of playful grazing and drinking is typically very brief, often less than a day. Once a foal begins ingesting the grass or drinking water, the playful, investigative form is not seen again. The foal may occasionally play with an unusual piece of vegetation, for example, a tall weed encountered while grazing.

An interesting feature of play, particularly in young foals, is that typically sequences do not include the vocalization included in the serious adult form of the behavior, with the exception of frolic. For example, play fighting does not include the grunts and squeals so typical of serious fighting. As reported by Fagen (1977), vocalizations of young foals (approximately three months of age and younger) are almost exclusively limited to calls and answers to the dam. When frolicking, pony and horse foals may snort and emit audible squeals. The development of play in domestic foals has been well described by Sharon Crowell-Davis (Crowell-Davis and Caudle 1989).

Play has been classified here into four major categories similar to classifications proposed for mammals in general (Fagen 1981). These include object play, play sexual behavior, locomotor play, and play fighting. Another distinction often made in the literature concerns social and solitary forms of play.

OBJECT PLAY

Object play involves contact and manipulation of an object. The target object may be either inanimate, such as an environmental object, or animate, such as the mane, tail, or other body part of a herd mate or even of an animal of another species. Object play has also been called *object manipulation* or *manipulative play* (Crowell-Davis 1986, Crowell-Davis et al. 1987, Waring 1983).

Some of these behaviors, for example *circle* and *to and from*, obviously involve locomotion. Although they could easily be classified as locomotor play, they so clearly seem focused on an object and often appear to be stimulated by the object. Accordingly, they are classified here with object play.

Nibble

With jaws closed, the upper lip is moved upward and downward against an object, typically without dental contact of the object.

Comments: *Nibbling* of an object is typically one of the first play responses associated with an investigative approach of the object. In many instances *nibbling* appears to be a means of moving an object on the ground.

Described in:

Horses — semi-feral ponies (Tyler 1972); free-ranging Appaloosa horses (Blakeslee 1974); feral horses (Waring 1983); feral ponies (Keiper 1985); Welsh pony mare and foal groups (Crowell-Davis 1983, 1986; Crowell-Davis et al. 1987)

Donkeys — feral asses *Equus africanus* (Moehlman 1974, 1998)

Young foal *nibbling* lilac branch

251

Sniff/Lick/Nuzzle

Inhalation with muzzle positioned near the object while inhaling (sniff). The muzzle and lips may contact the object. The tongue is extended through the teeth and border of the mouth, making contact with an object. It is then retracted into the mouth and chewing may follow.

Comments: *Sniffing, licking,* and/or *nuzzling* an inanimate object may be done to investigate the odor, texture, shape, taste, and size of an object. *Sniffing* and *licking* of a herd mate sometimes precede and appear to initiate mutual grooming.

Described in:

Horses — feral ponies (Keiper 1985)
Donkeys — semi-feral donkeys (J Beach unpublished observations)

Foal *licking* novel object (chair)

AMY POULIN

252

Two-year-old colt *sniffing* **and** *nuzzling* **novel object (camera tripod)**

SUE MCDONNELL

AMY POULIN

Foal *sniffing* **observer's shoe**

Mouth

Taking an object or part of an object into the mouth with upper and lower lips and tongue then placing it between the lips, incisors (front teeth), or molars. The head is usually elevated once the object is in the mouth (see *pick up*). The animal may move around with the object in the mouth (see *carry*).

Other Names: *manipulate by mouth* (Waring 1983).

Comments: The animal may shake the object by tossing the head and neck while the object is being mouthed. A dam's mane or tail is a common target of mouthing or chewing.

Described in:

Horses — free-ranging Appaloosa horses (Blakeslee 1974); domestic and feral horses and ponies (Waring 1983); Welsh pony foals and mares (Crowell-Davis 1983, 1986; Crowell-Davis et al. 1987)

Przewalski horses — zoo-managed Przewalski horses (Boyd and Houpt 1994)

Donkeys — feral asses *Equus africanus* (Moehlman 1974, 1998)

Foal *mouthing* novel object (camera tripod)

Chew

Side-to-side grinding motion of upper and lower jaw on an object in the mouth. May include head tossing and/or forward movement of the tongue through the front teeth ending with the object falling out of the mouth.

Comments: This behavior appears to be for the purpose of investigating the texture, shape, and/or size of the object rather than for nourishment. The mother's mane and/or tail are common target objects for *chewing* or *mouthing* by the foal. In horses and ponies, all ages have been observed to chew inanimate or animate objects. (McDonnell and Poulin 2002).

Described in:

Horses — semi-feral ponies (Tyler 1972); domestic and feral horses and ponies (Waring 1983)

Donkeys — semi-feral donkeys (J Beach unpublished observations)

Pick Up

Holding an object between the lips, front teeth, or molars. The head is elevated with the object in the mouth so that the object is lifted from the ground. The height at which the object is lifted can vary from a few inches to several feet.

Other Names: *lift* (Waring 1983).

Described in:

Horses — semi-feral ponies (Tyler 1972); domestic and feral horses and ponies (Waring 1983); Welsh pony foals and mares (Crowell-Davis 1983, 1986; Crowell-Davis et al. 1987)

Donkeys — feral asses *Equus africanus* (Moehlman 1974, 1998)

Foal *picking up* novel object (tissue paper)

Foal *picking up* small tree branch

AMY POULIN

Foal *picking up* field data sheet

Shake

Following *pick up*, movement of an object in a side-to-side, up-and-down, rotating, or circular motion.

Other Names: *scrape along ground* (Moehlman 1974, 1998); *wave about* (Crowell-Davis 1983); *swing head* (Crowell-Davis 1983; Crowell-Davis et al. 1987).

Described in:

Horses — Welsh pony foals and mares (Crowell-Davis 1983, 1986; Crowell-Davis et al. 1987)

Donkeys — feral asses *Equus africanus* (Moehlman 1974, 1998)

Social object play — foal *shaking* novel object (paper bag)

Carry

Following *pick up*, movement forward with the object held in the mouth.

Other names: *drag* (Moehlman 1974, 1998; Crowell-Davis et al. 1987).

Described in:

Horses — Welsh pony foals and mares (Crowell-Davis 1983, 1986; Crowell-Davis et al. 1987)

Donkeys — feral asses *Equus africanus* (Moehlman 1974, 1998)

Solitary object play — young foal *carrying* novel object (paper bag)

259

Drop or Toss

Following *pick up*, the upper and lower jaws open to release the object (*drop*), or the nose is thrown upward as the object is released (*toss*). A toss may alternately be effected without *pick up* by using the muzzle to flip an object from the substrate into the air.

Comments: Crowell-Davis (1983) notes that Welsh pony foals have been observed tossing the mane and tail of their dam with their nose.

Described in:

Horses — semi-feral ponies (Tyler 1972); domestic and feral horses and ponies (Waring 1983); Welsh pony foals and mares (Crowell-Davis 1983, 1986; Crowell-Davis et al. 1987)

Donkeys — feral asses *Equus africanus* (Moehlman 1974, 1998)

Foal *dropping* lilac bloom

Pull

Holding of an object between the lips or front teeth, followed by a dragging motion of the object with forward-and-back or side-to-side movement. The head and neck or full body may move in any direction.

Other names: *drag* (Crowell-Davis et al. 1987).

Described in:

Horses — semi-feral ponies (Tyler 1972); domestic and feral horses and ponies (Waring 1983); Welsh pony mares and foals at pasture (Crowell-Davis 1983; Crowell-Davis et al. 1987); feral ponies (Keiper 1985)

Przewalski horses — zoo-managed Przewalski horses (Boyd and Houpt 1994)

Donkeys — semi-feral donkeys (J Beach unpublished observations)

Two-year-old colt *pulling* on novel object (camera tripod)

Foal *mouthing* and *pulling* briars

Paw

With an object as an apparent target, one foreleg is lifted off the ground slightly, extended quickly in a forward direction, followed by a backward, toe-dragging movement as if digging. The movement is typically repeated several times in succession. The foot may have direct contact with the object, thus moving the object. Alternatively, the foot may be slightly behind the object, touching the ground.

Comments: Investigative sequences and water play typically include *pawing*. *Pawing* an animate object also occurs as an apparent play initiation gesture.

Described in:

Horses — semi-feral ponies (Tyler 1972); feral horses (Boyd 1980); domestic and feral horses (Waring 1983); Welsh pony mares and foals (Crowell-Davis 1983, 1986; Crowell-Davis et al. 1987); feral ponies (Keiper 1985)

Przewalski horses — zoo-managed Przewalski horses (Boyd and Houpt 1994)

Donkeys — feral asses *Equus africanus* (Moehlman 1974, 1998)

Foal and dam *pawing* in water

Foal *pawing* and *sniffing* (dropped tissue paper)

Yearling *pawing* observer's lunch bag

Foal *pawing* field data check sheets

AMY POULIN

Kick Up

Standing at right angles to a herd mate target (usually the dam), with the butt toward and often touching the abdomen of the target; weight is transferred to the forelegs as the hind legs, in a hopping motion, are raised a few inches off the ground toward the target. Typically no extension of the hind legs, as in kicking, occurs.

Described in:

Horses — semi-feral ponies (Tyler 1972); feral horses (Boyd 1980)
Donkeys — semi-feral donkeys (J Beach unpublished observations)
Zebra — Grevy's zebra *Equus grevyi* (Gardner 1983)

To and From

Locomotion, usually at a trot or gallop, away from an object, such as the dam or a tree, and then returning to the object at any gait.

Other names: runs in opposite directions (Moehlman 1974, 1998).

Comments: This behavioral sequence could also be considered as locomotor play but is classified here as object play because the action so obviously involves a landmark object.

Described in:

Horses — semi-feral ponies (Tyler 1972); pastured domestic ponies in natural herd (Fagen 1977); feral horses (Boyd 1980); domestic and feral horses and ponies (Waring 1983); feral ponies (Keiper 1985)

Donkeys — feral asses *Equus africanus* (Moehlman 1974, 1998)

Zebra — Grevy's zebra *Equus grevyi* (Gardner 1983)

Circle

Movement in a path, generally circular, around an object so that the beginning and ending points are in the same general vicinity. This behavior can be performed at any gait and may be repeated; can include stopping briefly and reversing direction of the circle.

Other names: *running in loops* (Blakeslee 1974).

Comments: *Circling* most frequently occurs in foals or adolescents and is rarely observed in mature animals. The focal animate object is usually the dam. A common inanimate focal object is a tall weed or tree. May also be classified as a locomotor behavior but included here with object play because of the distinct focus on an object.

Described in:

Horses — semi-feral ponies (Tyler 1972); free-ranging Appaloosa horses (Blakeslee 1974); feral horses (Boyd 1980); Welsh pony foals and mares (Crowell-Davis 1983, 1987); feral ponies (Keiper 1985)

Donkeys — semi-feral donkeys (J Beach unpublished observations)

Zebra — Grevy's zebra *Equus grevyi* (Gardner 1983)

Young foal *circling* dam

Resting Rear

One participant raises its chest and forelegs so that one or both limbs rest across the body of a herd mate, typically with lateral orientation.

Comments: The animal rearing may rotate around the partner's body so that the animals end up in the mounting position as for play sexual behavior (see page 273). In our observations of ponies, a considerable proportion of occurrences of *resting rear* are not within the context of sexual play per se but rather dispersed within bouts of locomotor play and play fighting.

Described in:

Horses — semi-feral ponies (Tyler 1972); free-ranging Appaloosa horses (Blakeslee 1974); domestic Shetland and Welsh pony mares and foals at pasture (Schoen et al. 1976); feral ponies (Keiper 1985)

Donkeys — feral asses *Equus africanus* (Moehlman 1974, 1998)

***Resting rear* between yearling playmates**

PLAY SEXUAL BEHAVIOR

Sexual play is conspicuous and frequent in foals and young adolescents of both sexes and among young and adult bachelor stallions. The elements of the precopulatory and copulatory sequences may be out of order or exaggerated from that of a mature adult in a breeding context. The following three entries represent commonly observed play sexual behavior in equids.

Elimination Marking Sequence

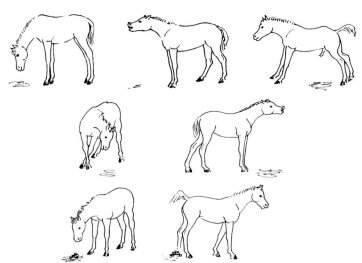

A sequence in which an animal approaches and sniffs voided urine or feces, performs the Flehmen response, covers the urine or feces with urine and/or feces, and then sniffs again and performs Flehmen response in the stylized postures typical of a mature stallion but in less organized sequences.

Comments: Usually performed by foals and more frequently by yearlings after elimination by a mature animal. Sequence is often quite similar to adult form except that it may not proceed in the order typical of adult elimination marking sequence and the elements may be interspersed among play sequences of other types, for example *frolic*.

Described in:

Horses — feral horses (Feist 1971); semi-feral ponies (Tyler 1972); free-ranging Appaloosa horses (Blakeslee 1974); Shetland and Welsh pony mares and foals at pasture (Schoen et al. 1976); feral ponies (Keiper 1985)

Przewalski horses — zoo-managed Przewalski horses (Boyd and Houpt 1994)

Donkeys — semi-feral donkeys (J Beach unpublished observations)

Tease

Sniffing, licking, and/or nuzzling another's head, shoulder, abdomen, flank, inguinal area, tail, and/or genital areas in a similar but more playful manner to that of an adult stallion investigating a mare before copulation.

Comments: Foals of both sexes and particularly yearling colts often tease a mare during or following a mature stallion's teasing or breeding of the mare. The precopulatory sequence may or may not be complete or in the order typical of a stallion. In play sequences, the *Flehmen response* occurs but the tip of the nose is typically not raised as high as a mature stallion's (Keiper 1985).

Described in:

Horses — semi-feral domestic ponies (Tyler 1972); free-ranging Appaloosa horses (Blakeslee 1974); Shetland and Welsh pony mares and foals at pasture (Schoen et al. 1976); feral ponies (Keiper 1985)

Zebra — Grevy's zebra *Equus grevyi* (Gardner 1983)

Tease

Foals play *teasing* sequence

Mount

Raising of the chest and forelegs onto the back of a herd mate (same or opposite sex) as during copulation in mature adults. The mount may be oriented from the side or rear.

Other names: *sexual mounting of mother* (Blakeslee 1974); *sex without coition* (McFarland 1987).

Comments: Usually performed by foals and immature young of both sexes to their mother and other immature herd mates. It may occur with or without precopulatory (teasing, elimination marking) or copulatory (thrusting) behavioral elements. Sexual arousal as in an adult is usually not apparent although erection can be present. Lateral *mount*, though similar in form to *resting rear*, appears distinct by context and form from *resting rear*. An abbreviated form of the mount may include only resting the chin and head on the hindquarters of the target animal (as if about to mount).

Described in:

Horses — feral horses (Feist 1971); semi-feral ponies (Tyler 1972); free-ranging Appaloosa horses (Blakeslee 1974); Shetland and Welsh pony mares and foals at pasture (Schoen et al. 1976); feral horses (Boyd 1980); domestic horse (Fagen 1981); domestic and feral horses and ponies (Waring 1983); Welsh pony foals and mare groups (Crowell-Davis 1983, 1986; Crowell-Davis et al. 1987); feral ponies (Keiper 1985)

Przewalski horses — zoo-managed Przewalski horses (Boyd and Houpt 1994)

Donkeys — feral asses *Equus africanus* (Moehlman 1974, 1998)

Zebra — Grevy's zebra *Equus grevyi* (Gardner 1983); Cape Mountain zebra *Equus zebra zebra* (Penzhorn 1984)

Mount

AMY POULIN

Male foal *mounting* another male foal from side (1) and from rear (2,3) (Note commencing erection.)

LOCOMOTOR PLAY

Locomotor play involves any play behavior response or sequence that is performed while in motion at any gait. *Circling* and *to and from* were included in object play because the action appears to be directed toward or around an object(s), but each can also be considered locomotor play.

With the exception of *chase* and *king of the mountain,* each of these locomotor play behaviors can occur either in a solitary or social context.

Frolic

Forelegs and hind legs simultaneously propelled off the ground along with apparently exuberant, random bucking, head shaking, and body twists. May take off from a stationary position to an instantaneous gallop.

Other names: *prop* (Fagen 1977); *cavorting* (Fagen 1981); *gamboling* (Fagen 1981, McFarland 1987).

Comments: May interrupt an episode of running.

Described in:

Horses — domestic pony foals pastured in a natural herd (Fagen 1977); domestic horse foals at pasture with dams (Fagen 1981); domestic and feral horses and ponies (Waring 1983); Welsh pony foals and mares (Crowell-Davis 1983; Crowell-Davis et al. 1987)

Donkeys — feral asses *Equus africanus* (Moehlman 1974, 1998)

Zebra — Grevy's zebra *Equus grevyi* (Gardner 1983)

Young foal *frolicking*

AMY POULIN

276

Run

With no apparent destination to reach or threat to escape, forward movement at the canter or gallop in a seemingly spontaneous burst of motion.

Other names: *galloping* (Tyler 1972, Keiper 1985); *exuberant galloping* (Waring 1983).

Comments: Fagen (1977) reported that greater than two-thirds of all running in pastured pony foals from birth to six weeks was in a play context.

Described in:

Horses — feral horses (Feist 1971); semi-feral ponies (Tyler 1972); free-ranging Appaloosa horses (Blakeslee 1974); Shetland and Welsh pony mares and foals at pasture (Schoen et al. 1976); domestic pony foals pastured in a natural herd (Fagen 1977); domestic horse foals with mares (Fagen 1981); domestic and feral horses and ponies (Waring 1983); Welsh pony mare and foal groups (Crowell-Davis 1983; Crowell-Davis et al. 1987); feral ponies (Keiper 1985); feral horses (Berger 1986)

Przewalski horses — zoo-managed Przewalski horses (Boyd and Houpt 1994)

Donkeys — feral asses *Equus africanus* (Moehlman 1974, 1998)

Zebra — Grevy's zebra *Equus grevyi* (Gardner 1983)

Foal solitary *running*

Chase

Rapid pursuit of a cohort at the trot, canter, or gallop with the apparent effort to catch up to and/or overtake it.

Other names: *race* (Penzhorn 1984); *charge* (Keiper 1985).

Comments: The animal often attempts to *nip* or bump (similar to *push* at speed) the pursued play partner while chasing. The participants may reverse roles of *chasing* and being pursued. Play *chasing* can occur as what appears to be simple locomotor "games" or "tag" or can occur within the context of play fighting. *Chasing*, particularly in play among bachelors, can also appear to be *herding* similar to that of a harem stallion herding and driving his mares (McDonnell and Haviland 1995).

Described in:

Horses — feral horses (Feist 1971); semi-feral ponies (Tyler 1972); free-ranging Appaloosa horses (Blakeslee 1974); Shetland and Welsh pony mares and foals at pasture (Schoen et al. 1976); domestic ponies pastured in a natural herd (Fagen 1977); feral horses (Boyd 1980); domestic and feral horses and ponies (Waring 1983); immature male feral horses (Hoffmann 1985); feral ponies (Keiper 1985); feral horses of the Great Basin (Berger 1986)

Przewalski horses — zoo-managed Przewalski horses (Boyd and Houpt 1994)

Yearling group *chase*

Donkeys — semi-feral donkeys (J Beach unpublished observations)

Zebra — Cape Mountain zebra *Equus zebra zebra* (Penzhorn 1984)

278

Buck

With the head and neck lowered and the weight shifted to the forelegs, both hind legs lift off the ground with simultaneous backward extension, often repeatedly in rapid succession.

Other names: *kicking of hind legs into the air* (Feist 1971); *kick out* (Tyler 1972, Fagen 1981); *kicking up* (Blakeslee 1974); *rear kicking* (Fagen 1981).

Described in:

Horses — feral horses (Feist 1971); semi-feral ponies (Tyler 1972); free-ranging Appaloosa horses (Blakeslee 1974); Shetland and Welsh pony mares and foals at pasture (Schoen et al. 1976); domestic ponies pastured in a natural herd (Fagen 1977); feral horses (Boyd 1980); domestic horse foals at pasture with dams (Fagen 1981); domestic and feral horses and ponies (Waring 1983); Welsh pony mare and foal groups (Crowell-Davis 1983, 1986; Crowell-Davis et al. 1987); feral ponies (Keiper 1985); feral horses (Berger 1986)

AMY POULIN

Foal *bucking*

Przewalski horses — zoo-managed Przewalski horses (Boyd and Houpt 1994)

Donkeys — feral asses *Equus africanus* (Moehlman 1974, 1998)

Zebra — Grevy's zebra *Equus grevyi* (Gardner 1983)

279

Jump

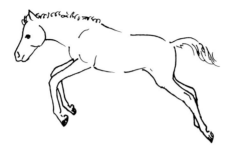

With mostly hind-leg propulsion, sudden movement forward with the forelegs leaving the ground first followed by the hind legs. Can appear to be jumping over a target obstacle or not.

Described in:

Horses — semi-feral ponies (Tyler 1972); domestic horse foals at pasture with dams (Fagen 1981); domestic and feral horses and ponies (Waring 1983)

Donkeys — feral asses *Equus africanus* (Moehlman 1974, 1998)

Young foal *jumping* over weeds

AMY POULIN

280

Leap

In a combination of *jump* and *frolic*, propulsion off the ground with fore and hind legs over an object, away from an object, or toward an object.

Comments: In the context of foal locomotor play and play as an adult, leap can sometimes resemble *frolic*; however the leap action is directed toward or against another animal (Fagen 1981; Crowell-Davis 1983, 1986; McFarland 1987).

Described in:

Horses — domestic horse foals (Fagen 1981); Welsh pony foals and mares (Crowell-Davis 1983, 1986; Crowell-Davis et al. 1987)

Donkeys — feral asses *Equus africanus* (Moehlman 1974, 1998)

Young foal *leaping*

Prance

Walk or trot forward with neck arched, ears forward, tail elevated, and knee action exaggerated. The head and neck may bob up and down while in motion and a snorting sound may be emitted with each stride.

Comments: Often occurs at the end of a play bout.

Described in:

Horses — semi-feral ponies (Tyler 1972); free-ranging Appaloosa horses (Blakeslee 1974); feral horses (Boyd 1980); Welsh pony mare and foal groups (Crowell-Davis 1983, 1986; Crowell-Davis et al. 1987); feral ponies (Keiper 1985)

Day-old foal *prancing*

King of the Mountain

In play groups, one or more playmates attaining and holding position at peak of small mounds. Individuals may alternate periods of holding the top position.

Comments: Often occurs at the end of a play bout.

Described in:

Horses — domestic horse foals (S Ralston personal communication 1999)

Donkeys — semi-feral donkeys (J Beach unpublished observations)

PLAY FIGHTING

Play fighting involves behavioral elements and sequences similar to serious adult fighting behavior but with more of a sporting character than serious fighting. In contrast to serious fights, the cohorts appear to alternate offensive and defensive roles, spar on as if to "keep the game going," and stop short of injury.

Initiation of play fighting has been observed to follow the head threat tossing motion in which the head is rapidly flipped up and down either while the animal is standing still or moving. Play fighting has been described in some detail by Berger (1986), Keiper (1985), Moehlman (1974, 1998), and Schilder et al. (1984). Play fighting has also been termed interactive (contact or combat) play (Crowell-Davis 1983, 1986; Crowell-Davis et al. 1987) and aggressive play (Tyler 1972).

For the behaviors involving mouth aggression, three types of action can be distinguished. The term *nip* is used to refer to a slight opening of the jaw to take and quickly release small pieces of skin or flesh between the teeth; *bite* to refer to a wider opening of the jaws and teeth to take and quickly release a larger piece of flesh and skin between the teeth; and *grasp* to refer to an extended clamping hold of a larger piece of flesh and skin, or a limb, between widely opened jaws.

Most play fighting occurs in a social context. However, certain elements such as *stamp* and *rear* occur also within solitary play bouts of young foals.

Head/Neck/Chest Nip and Bite

Nip: Jaws and teeth are opened and closed slightly while taking a small piece of hair or flesh of a cohort between the teeth.

Bite: Jaws and teeth are opened widely and closed on a large piece of flesh and skin of a cohort, then quickly released. The ears are upright and lips may be retracted.

Other names: *face nip* (Blakeslee 1974); *neck biting* (Gardner 1983).

Comments: Nipping and biting may occur in various areas of the body, including the fore body, the stifle, and flank.

Described in:

Horses — semi-feral ponies (Tyler 1972); free-ranging Appaloosa horses (Blakeslee 1974); Shetland and Welsh pony mares and foals at pasture (Schoen et al. 1976); domestic and feral horses and ponies (Waring 1983); feral ponies (Keiper 1985)

Przewalski horses — zoo-managed Przewalski horses (Boyd and Houpt 1994).

AMY POULIN

Foal *nipping* chest of cohort during play initiation

Donkeys — feral asses *Equus africanus* (Moehlman 1974, 1998)

Zebra — Grevy's zebra *Equus grevyi* (Gardner 1983); Cape Mountain zebra *Equus zebra zebra* (Penzhorn 1984)

Head/Neck/Chest Nip and Bite

Yearling *nipping* face of cohort

***Biting* face in play fight between two-year-old companions**

Neck Grasp

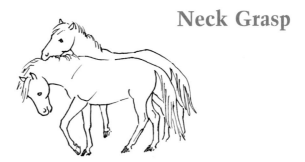

With the jaws open and clamped, holding of the mane and neck of a cohort at the crest and sometimes moving back and forth.

Other names: holding mane (Feist 1971); *neck grip* (Tyler 1972, Boyd 1980); *biting* (Moehlman 1974, 1998); *mane grip* (Schoen et al. 1976); *holding crest* (Crowell-Davis 1983); *grip neck or mane* (Keiper 1985); *grasp* (McDonnell and Haviland 1995) .

Comments: May precede (as if to initiate) or follow (as if initiated by) *mutual grooming* (S McDonnell unpublished observations, ponies).

Described in:

Horses — feral horses (Feist 1971); semi-feral ponies (Tyler 1972); Shetland and Welsh pony mares and foals at pasture (Schoen et al. 1976); feral horses (Boyd 1980); domestic horse mare and foal groups (Fagen 1981); Welsh pony mare and foal groups (Crowell-Davis 1983; Crowell-Davis et al. 1987); immature male feral horses (Hoffmann 1985); feral ponies (Keiper 1985); feral horses (Berger 1986); semi-feral bachelor bands (McDonnell and Haviland 1995)

Donkeys — feral asses *Equus africanus* (Moehlman 1974, 1998)

Zebra — Cape Mountain zebra *Equus zebra zebra* (Penzhorn 1984); Plains zebra *Equus quagga* (Berger 1986)

Neck grasp **during** *resting rear*

Neck Wrestle

Sparring with the head and neck. One or both partners may remain standing, drop to one or both knees, or raise the forelegs during a bout of *neck wrestling*. This activity may include pushing and slamming with the shoulder against the shoulder or abdomen of the partner.

Other names: *wrestle* (Hoffmann 1985); *neck fencing* (Berger 1986).

Described in:

Horses — feral horses (Feist 1971); semi-feral ponies (Tyler 1972); free-ranging Appaloosa horses (Blakeslee 1974); Shetland and Welsh pony mares and foals at pasture (Schoen et al. 1976); feral horses (Boyd 1980); domestic horse groups (Fagen 1981); immature male feral horses (Hoffmann 1985); feral ponies (Keiper 1985); feral horses (Berger 1986)

Donkeys — feral asses *Equus africanus* (Moehlman 1974, 1998)

Zebra — Cape Mountain zebra *Equus zebra zebra* (Penzhorn 1984)

Young foal and yearling *neck wrestling*

Foreleg Nip/Bite/Grasp

Nip: Jaws and teeth open and quickly close on a small amount of hair or skin of a foreleg of the target animal, then release.

Bite: Jaws and teeth open and close on a large portion of flesh of the target animal.

Grasp: Clamping of jaws and teeth in an extended hold on the limb of the target animal.

Comments: Typically causes the recipient to buckle at the knees and partially drop to the ground with the front end in an attempt to evade continued contact. Participants may continue nipping each other from the ground position.

Described in:

Horses — semi-feral ponies (Tyler 1972); free-ranging Appaloosa horses (Blakeslee 1974); Shetland and Welsh pony mares and foals at pasture (Schoen et al. 1976); domestic and feral horses and ponies (Waring 1983); feral ponies (Keiper 1985); feral horses of the Great Basin (Berger 1986); Welsh pony foal and mare groups (Crowell-Davis 1986).

Przewalski horses — zoo-managed Przewalski horses (Boyd and Houpt 1994)

Donkeys — semi-feral donkeys (J Beach unpublished observations)

Zebra — Cape Mountain zebra *Equus zebra zebra* (Penzhorn 1984); Plains zebra *Equus quagga* (Berger 1986)

Foreleg Nip/Bite/Grasp

Foal *grasping* foreleg of yearling cohort

Young stallions *biting* and *grasping* forelegs

Hind Leg Nip/Bite/Grasp

Nip: Jaws and teeth open and quickly close on a small amount of hair or skin of a hind leg of the opposing participant, then release.

Bite: Jaws and teeth open and close on a large portion of flesh of the target animal.

Grasp: Jaws and teeth open and clamp in an extended hold of the limb of the play partner.

Comments: Mutual hind leg *nipping, biting,* and *grasping* typically lead to circling of two participants in an apparent attempt to avoid being bitten while continuing to bite.

Described in:

Horses — semi-feral ponies (Tyler 1972); free-ranging Appaloosa horses (Blakeslee 1974); Shetland and Welsh pony mares and foals at pasture (Schoen et al. 1976); domestic and feral horses and ponies (Waring 1983); feral ponies (Keiper 1985)

Przewalski horses — zoo-managed Przewalski horses (Boyd and Houpt 1994)

Donkeys — semi-feral donkeys (J Beach unpublished observations)

Zebra — Cape Mountain zebra *Equus zebra zebra* (Penzhorn 1984)

Hind Leg Nip/Bite/Grasp

Young foal *grasping* hind leg of older foal

Older and younger foals circling as each *nips* or *bites*
the other's hind leg

292

Rump Nip or Bite

Jaws and teeth open and close, taking a small (*nip*) or large (*bite*) piece of flesh on the posterior section of the rump, then quickly releasing.

Comments: May be followed with a *buck* from the recipient. Schoen et al. (1976) note that tail biting is a component of play fighting.

Described in:

Horses — semi-feral ponies (Tyler 1972); free-ranging Appaloosa horses (Blakeslee 1974); domestic and feral horses and ponies (Waring 1983); feral ponies (Keiper 1985)

Przewalski horses — zoo-managed Przewalski horses (Boyd and Houpt 1994)

Donkeys — semi-feral donkeys (J Beach unpublished observations)

Zebra — Cape Mountain zebra *Equus zebra zebra* (Penzhorn 1984)

Stamp

One foreleg raised and lowered, sharply and firmly striking the ground, sometimes repeated in a quick burst typically within the context of a play fight sequence. May serve to emit an acoustical signal.

Other names: *paw* (Schoen et al. 1976); *strike* (Boyd 1980, Crowell-Davis 1983, Waring 1983); *front hoof beating* (Hoffmann 1985); *stomp* (McDonnell and Haviland 1995).

Described in:

Horses — Shetland and Welsh mares and foals at pasture (Schoen et al. 1976); feral horses (Boyd 1980); domestic and feral horses and ponies (Waring 1983); Welsh pony mare and foal groups (Crowell-Davis 1983); immature male groups of feral horses (Hoffmann 1985)

Push

Head, neck, shoulders, chest, body, or rump pressed against the play partner in an apparent attempt to displace the other. Sometimes in a single episode two participants alternate roles of pushing and being pushed.

Other names: *bump against* (Gardner 1983); *push and bunt* (Crowell-Davis 1986).

Described in:

Horses — feral horses (Feist 1971); domestic and feral horses and ponies (Waring 1983); Welsh pony mares and foals (Crowell-Davis 1983, 1986; Crowell-Davis et al. 1987); feral horses (Berger 1986)

Donkeys — semi-feral donkeys (J Beach unpublished observations)

Zebra — Grevy's zebra *Equus grevyi* (Gardner 1983)

Young foal *pushing*

Rear

Fore quarters are raised high while the hind legs remain on the ground, resulting in a near-vertical position.

Comments: May result in the *resting rear* position or the *partial mount* or *dancing* or *boxing* (McDonnell and Haviland 1995). Commonly interpreted as related to establishment of dominance during a play fight sequence.

Described in:

Horses — semi-feral ponies (Tyler 1972); free-ranging Appaloosa horses (Blakeslee 1974); Shetland and Welsh mare and foals at pasture (Schoen et al. 1976); domestic ponies pastured in a natural herd (Fagen 1977); feral horses (Boyd 1980); domestic horse groups (Fagen 1981); domestic and feral horses and ponies (Waring 1983); Welsh pony mare and foal groups (Crowell-Davis 1983, 1986; Crowell-Davis et al. 1987); semi-feral ponies (Keiper 1985); feral horses (Berger 1986).

Przewalski horses — zoo-managed Przewalski horses (Boyd and Houpt 1994)

Donkeys — feral asses *Equus africanus* (Moehlman 1974, 1998)

Zebra — Cape Mountain zebra *Equus zebra zebra* (Penzhorn 1984)

AMY POULIN

Rear with ***dancing*** (within a play fighting sequence of young adult male ponies)

Hindquarter Threat

Usually with ears back and the rump turned toward a herd mate, raising of one leg as if aiming to kick, often simultaneously backing toward the target.

Other names: *kick threat* (McDonnell and Haviland 1995).

Comments: May occur in the context of a play fight sequence; sometimes appearing to signal the termination of the play fight (Keiper 1986).

Described in:

Horses — free-ranging Appaloosa horses (Blakeslee 1974); domestic and feral horses and ponies (Waring 1983)

Donkeys — feral asses *Equus africanus* (Moehlman 1974, 1998)

Zebra — Cape Mountain zebra *Equus zebra zebra* (Penzhorn 1984)

Foal hindquarter *threatening* cohorts (behind out of view) while guarding novel object (tissue paper)

Kick

Lifting of one hind leg off the ground and extending backward, usually toward the play partner, rarely with sufficient reach or force to touch or cause injury to the recipient. May be repeated in succession.

Other names: *kick out* (Tyler 1972, Gardner 1983); *hind kicking* (Boyd 1980).

Comments: A double hind-leg kick seems more forceful than play, and often seems to terminate the play fight sequence, so may not represent play.

Described in:

Horses — semi-feral ponies (Tyler 1972); feral horses (Boyd 1980); domestic and feral horses and ponies (Waring 1983); Welsh pony mare and foal groups (Crowell-Davis et al. 1987)

Przewalski horses — zoo-managed Przewalski horses (Boyd and Houpt 1994)

Donkeys — feral asses *Equus africanus* (Moehlman 1974, 1998)

Zebra — Grevy's zebra
Equus grevyi
(Gardner 1983); Cape
Mountain zebra
Equus zebra zebra
(Penzhorn 1984)

Foal *threatening to kick* in play with cohort

Evasive Balk

As two cohorts approach, one stopping abruptly, reversing direction of the fore body, typically withdrawing the head and neck (and sometimes fore body) in a sweeping dorsolateral motion while the hind body remains or pivots in place.

Other names: *quick stop* (Moehlman 1974, 1998); *swerving* (Waring 1983).

Described in:

Horses — semi-feral pony bachelor bands (McDonnell and Haviland 1995)

Donkeys — feral asses *Equus africanus* (Moehlman 1974, 1998)

Evasive Jump

During social locomotor play and play fighting, avoiding of a cohort by propelling the fore, rear, or entire body off the ground away from the offensive gesture.

Comments: In a given sequence, play opponents often alternate evading and attacking roles.

Described in:

Horses — free-ranging Appaloosa horses (Blakeslee 1974); feral ponies (Keiper 1985)

Donkeys — semi-feral donkeys (J Beach unpublished observations)

Evasive Spin

During social locomotor play and play fighting, avoiding contact by turning away from the offensive gesture in a quick, sharp motion pivoting around one hind leg.

Other names: *whirling to avoid being bitten* (Boyd 1980).

Described in:

Horses — feral horses (Boyd 1980); Welsh pony mare and foal groups (Crowell-Davis 1983; Crowell-Davis et al. 1987); domestic and feral horses and ponies (Waring 1983)

Donkeys — semi-feral donkeys (J Beach unpublished observations)

Foal *evasive spin*

Examples of Play Initiation

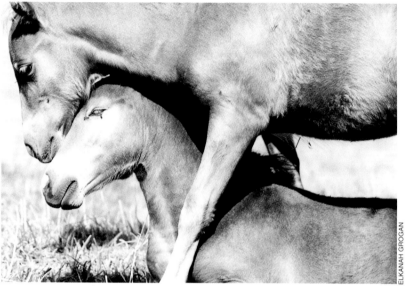

Young colt *initiating play* by straddling recumbent playmate

***Mutual grooming*, in this instance preceding social play bout**

302

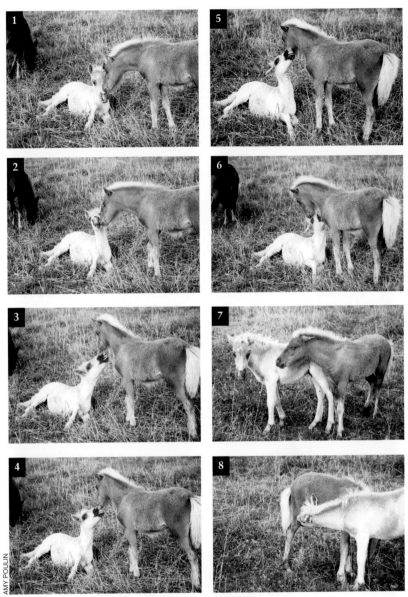

AMY POULIN

**Play initiation and teasing sequence
between young foal play mates**

Foal initiating play by *biting hock* and *pulling tail* of yearling

SUE MCDONNELL

DOMESTICALLY
SHAPED
AND
ABERRANT
BEHAVIORS

Just as with any domestic species, there are many behavioral marvels inherent to management and training of horses. One of those marvels is the trainability of horses to comply with human direction and modification of their behavior. The wide range of work and performance tasks of horses is truly remarkable — from dragging logs to pulling people on skis, cutting cattle, working as police assistants in crowd control, jumping, working together as a team or four-in-hand, and negotiating hazards in event driving. Training horses to accomplish such tractability and service includes extinguishing certain natural intra- and inter-species behaviors, for example flight and aggressive and sexual behaviors. Training also involves gradually shaping, directing, and modifying inherent species typical behavior to produce extraordinary sport, show, and performance behavior.

Traditional methods of training horses have varied from frank cruelty to positive reinforcement-based shaping of behavior that builds trust and willingness to comply with extraordinary requests. A recently published history of horse training methods from the days of the first domestic horses to modern time makes for very interesting reading (Richardson 1998).

Standing stalls for horses parked in harness

Another marvel is the extreme behavioral flexibility of horses in general and as individuals over a lifetime to adapt to a wide range of management and conditions. Both within and between agricultural venues of the world, the housing, nutrition, social groupings, handling, training, breeding, and transportation of horses are widely diverse in terms of the behavior expected of the horse. For example, most horses do well adjusting to many different types of indoor housing arrangements (as shown in these photographs). This behavioral flexibility holds generally true even for horses captured as adults from feral stock that has run and bred under wild conditions for generations.

Just as interesting as the adaptability of horses to our domestic environments is the fact that domestic horses of stock that have been bred for a certain phenotype and sport or work for generations and pampered life-long by our husbandry revert to natural social organization when turned out to open space and fend extraordinarily well without our assistance or intervention. In all but the most severe barren physical environments, feral horses, as they are known, thrive and reproduce.

Group tie stalls

In spite of generally remarkable flexibility and adaptability to a variety of environments, a small percentage of domestic horses develop behavior problems that clearly appear to be related to physical, nutritional, or social environmental aspects of domestic management. By far the most common and troublesome behavior problems of domestic horses are repeated movements or stylized behavior sequences that seem aimless. These are called stereotypies (Houpt and McDonnell 1993). Estimates of the prevalence of these behaviors among domestic horses range from

Isolation box stall

about 5% to as high as 25%. Stereotypies are rarely, if ever, seen in equids born and kept in natural social and free-ranging conditions. Captive wild born equids have a very high incidence. The most common stereotypies are locomotor, including perimeter walking, weaving, pacing, and rhythmic head swaying, shaking, and bobbing movements. A peculiar stereotypy known as "cribbing" involves grasping onto a surface with the incisors and gulping in and then expelling air through the mouth. Horses also exhibit a form of self-mutilative stereotypic behavior, typically involving biting of the flank, hind limb, or chest, sometimes with kicking against objects. In addition, horses in domestic environments suffer a disproportionate frequency of health problems related to over feeding, reduced natural forage, reduced exercise, foot care issues, athletic injuries, social injuries, and other suboptimal features of domestic environments. So signs of discomfort and pain, while they certainly do occur under natural conditions, seem much more common among domestic horses.

This section includes examples of shaped and trained behaviors and of problem or aberrant behavior of domestically managed horses. It ends with examples of behavior of pain and discomfort seen more often in domestically managed horses than in feral and wild horses.

Schooled (Operantly Shaped) Behaviors

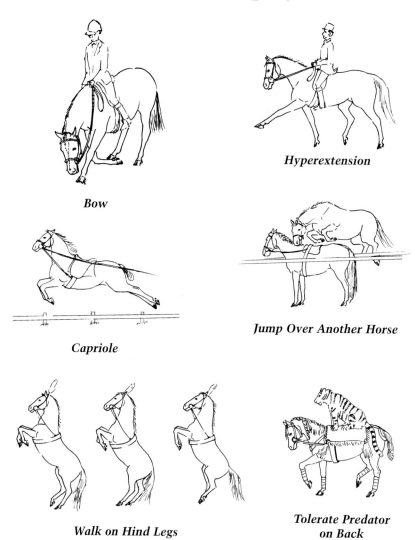

Bow

Hyperextension

Capriole

Jump Over Another Horse

Walk on Hind Legs

Tolerate Predator on Back

Performance movements achieved by operant shaping from natural behavioral elements.

Described in:

Horses — domestic horses and ponies (Waring 1983)

Schooled and Shaped Behaviors

Shaped performance behavior (Haflingers in Austria): vaulting (1), towing a land skier (2), and jumping (3)

ELKANAH GROGAN

309

Diverse Work and Performance Training

Examples of diverse work and performance training of horses: polo (1), kids pony racing (2), steeplechase racing (3), circus parading (4), and driving pair (5)

SUE MCDONNELL

SUE MCDONNELL

Schooled (Operantly Shaped) Behavior

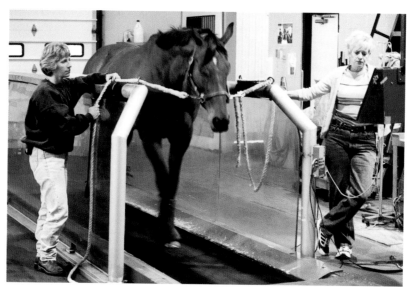

Treadmill training

Collection of semen for artificial insemination using a dummy mount

ELKANAH GROGAN

Well-trained Belgian breeding stallion loading in a stock trailer

SUE MCDONNELL

Learned Helplessness/ Submissive Posture

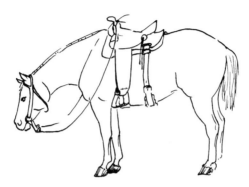

Standing quietly with head lowered, unresponsive to normal social and environmental stimuli, and moving only on release command or directive of the handler. Considered basic training in certain Western show and working disciplines.

Comments: Achieved using flooding and desensitization during immobilization.

Described in:

Horses — domestic horses and ponies (Miller 1974)

ABERRANT OR ANOMALOUS BEHAVIORS

Separation Anxiety

When separated from herd mates, frantic locomotor behavior, typically with long, loud whinny vocalizations. Pacing or frantic running may focus at the gate or fence line barrier, thwarting the animal from re-joining herd mates.

Other names: *isolation stress, herd bound.*

Comments: common between mares and foals, or stallions and their mares, but also can be extreme in certain other bonded individuals.

Described in:

Horses — domestic horses and ponies (S McDonnell unpublished observations)

Przewalski horses — zoo-managed Przewalski horses (Boyd and Houpt 1994)

Donkeys — domestic donkeys (J Beach unpublished observations)

Zebra — captive-bred Grevy's zebra *Equus grevyi* and Grant's zebra *Equus burchelli boehmi* (S McDonnell unpublished observations)

315

Mare frantically pacing and weaving when separated from herd mates

Chicken and horse companions (above) and cat and pony weanling companions

Cribbing

Unique equine aberrant behavior involving grasping of surface with incisors while arching the neck and drawing a gulp of air into the throat and then expelling it, repeated rhythmically in bouts typically lasting from minutes to as long as an hour.

Other names: *crib biting, wind sucking.*

Comments: Episodes often occur during and after grain feeding time.

Described in:

Horses — domestic horses and ponies (Waring 1983, McBane 1987, Fraser 1992).

Przewalski horses — zoo-managed Przewalski horses (Boyd and Houpt 1994)

Mare *cribbing* in spite of anti-cribbing collar

Horse *cribbing* on fence post

SUE MCDONNELL

Tongue Displacement

Tongue hanging far out of the mouth, usually to the side where it dangles loosely, sometimes moving from one side to the other. This tongue hanging can occur when under bit or at rest in stall or pasture.

Other names: *tongue waving, tongue dragging, tongue displacement* (Fraser 1992).

Comments: Often occurs during racing or eventing, where it does not appear to affect performance adversely.

Described in:

Horses — domestic horses and ponies (Waring 1983, Fraser 1992).

SUE ROSENBACH

Tongue displacement **in a racing horse**

Tongue Lolly

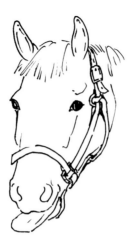

Extraneous moving of the tongue in and out of mouth.

Other names: *lick lipping, lapping.*

Comments: Sometimes occurs in association with *polydipsia.*

Described in:

Horses — domestic horses (S McDonnell unpublished observations)

Tongue Sucking

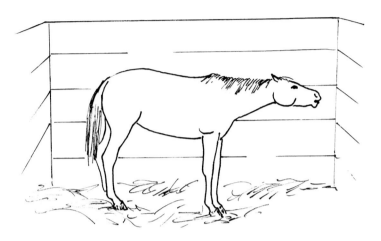

Sucking the tongue as a foal would suck a teat, typically with ears back and the neck and head extended level with the body or with the neck down and the head curved upward, typical of a foal reaching for the udder.

Other names: *non-nutritive sucking.*

Comments: Apparently more common among early weaned and orphaned, hand-fed foals.

Described in:

Horses — domestic horses (S McDonnell unpublished observations)

Non-nutritive Sucking

Sucking on own or herd mate's body as if sucking the dam's udder. Common self-targets are abdominal coat, prepuce, penis, hind leg. Herd mate targets also include ears, tail, and immature udder.

Other names: *inter-sucking, hair sucking.*
Described in:

Horses — domestic horses (S McDonnell unpublished observations)
Przewalski horses — London zoo-confined Przewalski 4-month-old weanlings (Boyd and Houpt 1994)

Perimeter Walking, Pacing, Circling

Stylized repetitious locomotion at any gait, usually along a perimeter.

Other names: *box-walking* (Prince 1987).

Described in:

Horses — domestic horses and ponies (Waring 1983, Prince 1987, Fraser 1992)

Przewalski horses — zoo-managed Przewalski horses (Boyd 1986, Boyd and Houpt 1994).

Donkeys — semi-feral donkeys (S McDonnell unpublished observations)

Zebra — captive-bred Grevy's zebra *Equus grevyi* and Grant's zebra *Equus burchelli boehmi* (S McDonnell unpublished observations)

Perimeter Walking, Pacing, Circling

Stallion *pacing* at a gate

SUE MCDONNELL

Stallion *walking* a pasture fence line

SUE MCDONNELL

Perimeter Walking, Pacing, Circling

Miniature horse stallion *circling* stall, and circular pattern
in straw bedding after hours of *circling*

Weaving

Abbreviated pacing involving rhythmic, repeated side-to-side shifting of the weight on the forelegs. The vigor and speed of movement vary among individuals and within or between episodes from slow to frenetic. The front feet may remain "planted" in position, or in an extreme form, the horse "throws" its fore body from one side to the other of a doorway or narrow stall, sometimes contacting the walls with each motion.

Other names: *swaying.*

Comments: Often begins as pacing, and over time or within an episode the travel shortens to simply throwing weight back and forth from one foreleg to the other.

Described in:

Horses — domestic horses and ponies (Waring 1983, Fraser 1992)

Przewalski horses — zoo-managed Przewalski horses (Boyd and Houpt 1994)

Stereotypic Pawing

Repetitive, seemingly aimless rhythmic dragging of a hoof in the same action as normal pawing, as is used in uncovering vegetation.

Described in:

Horses — domestic horses and ponies (Waring 1983, Fraser 1992)

Przewalski horses — zoo-managed Przewalski horses (KA Houpt personal communication)

Zebra — captive-bred Grevy's zebra *Equus grevyi* and Grant's zebra *Equus burchelli boehmi* (S McDonnell unpublished observations)

Stallion *pawing* while eating grain

Wall or Fence Kicking

Deliberate extension of the hind leg to contact barriers, using one or both hind legs alternately or simultaneously.

Described in:

Horses — domestic horses and ponies (Waring 1983, Fraser 1992)

Przewalski horses — zoo-managed Przewalski horses (Houpt 1994)

Stereotypic Stomping

Lifting and lowering of a hind leg as if deliberately striking the substrate, using one or both hind legs one at a time.

Other names: *knocking.*

Comments: Caretakers perceive the rhythmic noise produced by *stomping*, particularly on wooden or metal surfaces, to be the reinforcing goal of the behavior to the horse.

Described in:

Horses — domestic horses and ponies (Waring 1983, Fraser 1992)

Head Shaking, Bobbing, Tossing, Nodding (Stereotypic)

Mild Flipping Motion

"Yes" or Nodding Motion

Repeated, rhythmic head movements.

Other names: *nose-flipping.*

Comments: *Head shaking, bobbing, tossing,* and *nodding* are almost always attributable to physical pain or discomfort (such as allergies, ear parasites, neurologic disorders, dental problems).

Described in:

Horses — domestic horses and ponies (Waring 1983, McBane 1987, Fraser 1992)

Self-mutilation

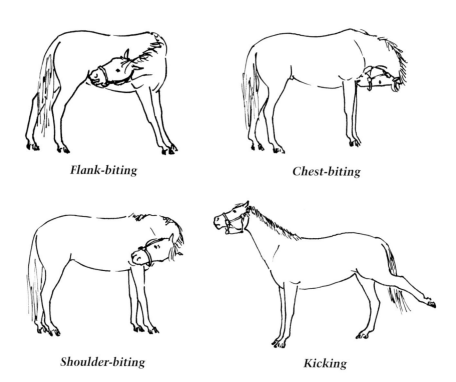

Flank-biting

Chest-biting

Shoulder-biting

Kicking

Repeated self-injury by biting, kicking, or lunging into objects.

Other names: *flank-biting.*

Comments: Can include violent spinning, vocalization.

Described in:

Horses — domestic horses and ponies (McDonnell 1986, Fraser 1992)

Przewalski horses — zoo-managed Przewalski horses (Houpt 1994)

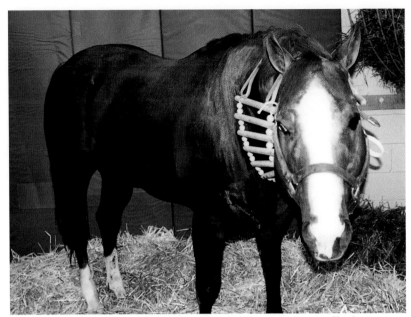

Self-mutilating Quarter Horse breeding stallion wearing cradle device to inhibit self-biting (note self-inflicted shoulder wound)

Self-mutilating breeding stallion biting flank

Inadequate Maternal Behavior

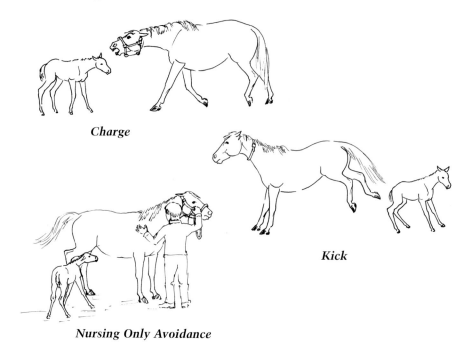

Charge

Kick

Nursing Only Avoidance

Attack or lack of normal tolerance of the neonate by the dam.

Other names: *mismothering, foal rejection* (Houpt, 1984, Houpt and Olm 1984).

Comments: There are several distinct types of maternal behavior problems. Some are related solely to nursing only and are often related to physical discomfort at the udder. Fear of the foal, as if it were unrecognized as the offspring, may occur in first-time mothers. Savage attack usually does not resolve, and the foal must be reared by alternative means, either fostered to a nurse mare or hand-fed. In confinement a mare's protective instinct may cause injury to the foal as the dam rushes to intervene between the foal and perceived threats.

Described in:

Horses — domestic horses and ponies (Houpt 1984, Chavatte 1991)

Wood Chewing

Chewing and/or ingesting wooden objects such as fences or stall construction materials.

Other names: *lignophagia* (Fraser 1992).

Comments: Woody browse is normal diet for wild horses. In domestic horses this behavior is believed to be related to a need for roughage in the diet. Concerns related to chewing and ingesting fences and building materials in domestic horses include digestive problems, property damage, and splinters. Horses will sometimes chew through a barrier with determination as if intending to escape.

Described in:

Horses — domestic horses and ponies (Waring 1983)

Przewalski horses — zoo-managed Przewalski horses (Boyd 1991, Boyd and Houpt 1994).

Donkeys — semi-feral donkeys (J Beach unpublished observations)

SUE MCDONNELL

Group of mares *chewing* and ingesting old wooden mineral feeder box

335

Pica

Ingestion of sand or soil in considerable quantity.

Other names: *soil-eating* (Fraser 1992), *geophagia* (McGreevy et al. 2001).

Comments: Commonly attributed to nutritional mineral deficiencies or to attractive contaminants of soil (McGreevy et al. 2001). Health concerns include gastrointestinal disorders.

Described in:

Horses — domestic horses and ponies (Waring 1983)

Coprophagy in Adults

Ingestion of feces.

Comments: Normal and common in young foals (see Coprophagy in Section IV, page 227). Rare in adults where it is attributed to severe nutritional deficiencies, lack of roughage or food.

Described in:

Horses — domestic horses and ponies (Waring 1983); starving feral horses (Feist and McCullough 1976)

Przewalski horses — captive Przewalski horses (Boyd and Houpt 1994)

Donkeys — semi-feral donkeys (J Beach unpublished observations)

Trichophagia

Ingestion of hair.

Other names: *tail chewing.*
Described in:

Horses — domestic horses and ponies (Waring 1983)

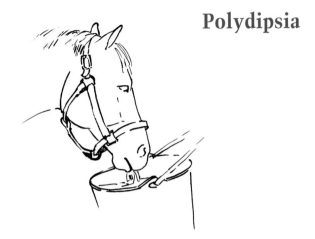

Polydipsia

Excessive ingestion of water.

Other names: *excessive drinking, polydipsia nervosa* (Fraser 1992).

Comments: Most commonly related to disease. Behavioral *polydipsia* usually includes significant playing or tongue lolling as opposed to simple drinking.

Described in:

Horses — domestic horses and ponies (Waring 1983); domestic horses (Fraser 1992)

Quidding

Dropping grain or partially chewed clump of forage from mouth while eating.

Comments: Related to dental problems (Waring 1983), mouth pain, or impaired tongue control as from bit damage (McBane 1987).

Described in:

Horses — domestic horses and ponies (Waring 1983); domestic horses (McBane 1987, Fraser 1992)

Hyperphagia

Aggressively "diving into" feed or hay, sometimes grabbing, gulping, and quickly swallowing large quantities, and/or pulling away quickly from the feed container.

Other names: *bolting feed* (McBane 1987), *hyperphagia nervosa* (Fraser 1992).

Comments: Health concerns include poor digestion because of rapid ingestion without adequate chewing. May have any of a number of apparent causes, including crowding or threatening herd mates at feeding time, with or without limited or protected feed supply; infrequent highly palatable concentrated meals.

Described in:

Horses — domestic horses (McBane 1987, Fraser 1992)

Donkeys — semi-feral donkeys (J Beach unpublished observations)

Food-related Aggression

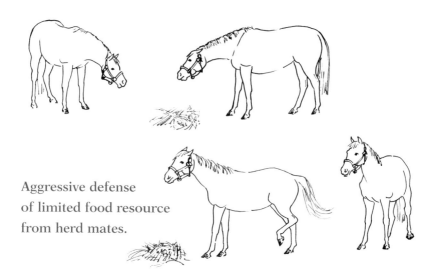

Aggressive defense
of limited food resource
from herd mates.

Comments: Associated with limited and spatially concentrated
food or water resources or highly palatable concentrated meals.
Aggressive protectiveness of food can be directed toward people.

Described in:

Horses — domestic horses and ponies (Waring 1983)

Przewalski horses — zoo-managed Przewalski horses (KA Houpt
personal communication)

Donkeys — semi-feral donkeys (J Beach unpublished observations)

**Gelding displacing pasture mate from his feed bucket with
simple *head threat***

Interspecies Sexual Behavior

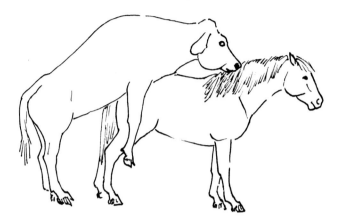

Sexual interaction with animal of another species.

Other names: *extra-specific sexual behavior.*

Comments: Horses have been observed interacting sexually with sheep, dogs, cattle, and llamas.

Described in:

Horses — domestic miniature horse stallion herding and mounting ewes; domestic horse mare soliciting and tolerating mounting by domestic cow; mare tolerating mounting by male llama (S McDonnell unpublished observations)

Donkeys — semi-feral donkeys (J Beach unpublished observations)

Pain and Discomfort

Colic

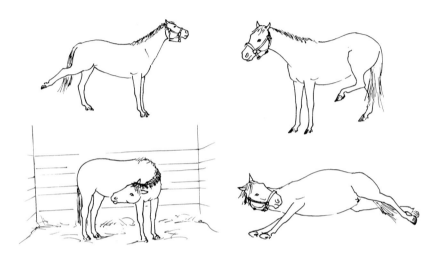

Behavior associated with gastrointestinal or other abdominal discomfort, including hind leg extension, drawing of a hind leg toward abdomen, gazing back at abdomen, recumbency, rolling, getting up and down, groaning.

Described in:

Horses — domestic horses and ponies (Waring 1983)

Przewalski horses — zoo-managed Przewalski horses (KA Houpt personal communication)

Donkeys — semi-feral donkeys (J Beach unpublished observations)

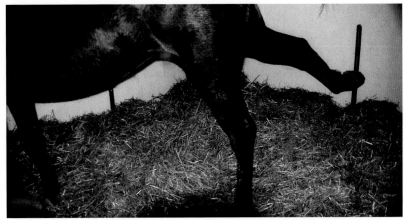

Mare kicking out, often contacting wall (In this case physical pain from an internal abscess was found to be the cause.)

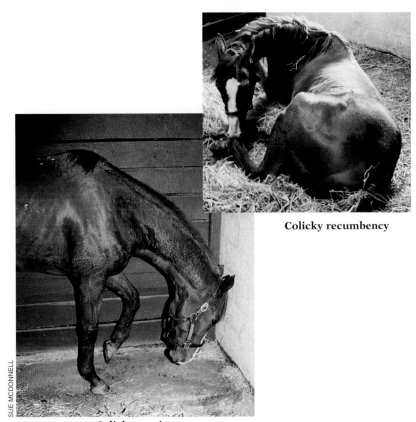

Colicky recumbency

SUE MCDONNELL

Colicky pawing

Founder

Behavior associated with painful feet, including shifting weight from affected limbs, lifting of affected limbs, and increased recumbency.

Other names: *laminitis.*

Described in:

Horses — domestic horses and ponies (Evans 1989, Waring 1983)

Przewalski horses — zoo-managed Przewalski horses (Houpt 1994)

Donkeys — semi-feral donkeys (J Beach unpublished observations)

Depression

Lethargic, dull, and quiet manner associated with physical illness, weakness, or severe social stress.

Described in:

Horses — domestic horses and ponies (Waring 1983)

Przewalski horses — zoo-confined Przewalski horses (S McDonnell unpublished observations)

Donkeys — semi-feral donkeys (J Beach unpublished observations)

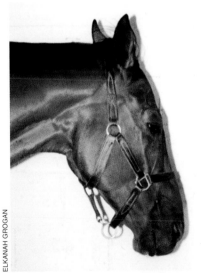

ELKANAH GROGAN

Gelding with expression typical of *depression* associated with physical discomfort

Head Press

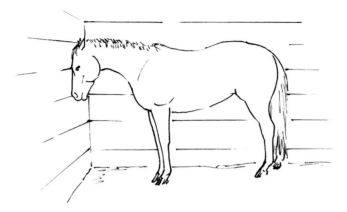

Pushing face against vertical surface; associated with central nervous system disease.

Comments: Indicates central nervous system problems.

Described in:

Horses — domestic horses and ponies (Waring 1983)

Donkeys — domestic donkeys (J Palmer unpublished observations)

Teeth Grind

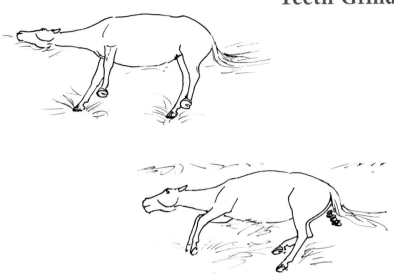

With jaws clenched, moving the jaws back and forth and rubbing the upper and lower teeth.

Described in:

Horses — domestic horses and ponies (Waring 1983, McBane 1987)

Donkeys — domestic donkeys (J Palmer unpublished observations)

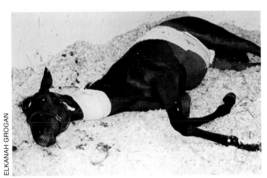

ELKANAH GROGAN

Young horse *teeth grinding* in association with apparent abdominal discomfort

GLOSSARY*

Aberrant behavior — abnormal behavior. Classic examples of aberrant behavior in domestic horses include the stereotypies (pacing, weaving, cribbing) and self-mutilation.

Abdomen — in equids, the lower part of the body between the shoulder and hip; belly.

Agonistic behavior — interactions among members of a herd that serve to establish and maintain social order, establish boundaries between subgroups, and access to limited resources, including aggression, threat, appeasement, avoidance responses, displays, and posturing rituals.

Aggressive behavior — fighting, attacking.

Alarm responses — highly stylized responses and postures to signs of danger that serve to alert the group. The responses typically provide auditory, olfactory, and/or visual signals to the group. Typical alarm signals in the horse are the alert stance with eyes and ears pointing toward the threat and the blow or snort vocalization.

Allogrooming — grooming of one herd mate by another, usually in areas of the body that are not easily reached with self-grooming; rarely seen in horses. More common in horses is **mutual grooming**, whereby two individuals simultaneously groom one another. (see Mutual grooming)

Ambivalent behavior — in a motivational conflict situation, the tendency to perform two incompatible activities. The animal may make intentional movements toward both activities. A commonly observed example of ambivalent behavior in horses under natural conditions is the estrus mare who momentarily vacillates from solicitous estrus to escape behavior. This ambivalence is often exaggerated under domestic breeding conditions where close confinement and handling for breeding appear to heighten the natural conflict between drive to breed and tendency to escape.

---

* This list of short definitions is one we have used for students and visitors to our lab who may not have yet formally studied animal behavior. In our lab, we rely heavily on David McFarland's quick reference book *The Oxford Companion to Animal Behavior* for more detailed introductory information. It contains concise explanations of key concepts in the study of animal behavior. Many of the definitions below, as they pertain to horses, were condensed from that valuable reference.

Animal welfare — as a discipline, the study of the physical and psychological health and well-being of domestic animal or wildlife populations under human control or supervision, or impacted by humans.

Animal well-being — the physical and psychological health of an animal, usually referring to animals under the care of humans.

Anthropomorphism — attributing human emotion, thought, or intentions to animals. This is considered unscientific because we have yet to determine the cognitive and emotional sophistication of animals.

Applied animal behavior (applied animal ethology) — the study of the behavior of domestic animals, considering both their natural behavior and their behavior under domestic conditions. Research and clinical applied animal behaviorists are interested in understanding effects of domestic management such as housing, nutrition, and social environment on behavior and well-being, as well as preventing and overcoming individual and herd behavior problems such as social incompatibilities, maternal behavior problems, aggression toward people, or sexual behavior dysfunction.

Appeasement — behavior that serves to inhibit or reduce aggression to gain acceptance among members of the same species, in situations where escape is impossible or disadvantageous. A conspicuous appeasement response seen often in horses is the *teeth clapping* or *champing* shown usually by young foals, but also seen in "cornered" adults, particularly stallions. (see Section II, General Social Communication)

Autogrooming — self-grooming, including rubbing, scratching, licking, and nipping.

Bachelor band — in equids, a relatively stable social group of non-harem males. Bachelor bands are usually associated with a larger herd including harem bands.

Band — in equids, a relatively stable social group. (see Social organization)

Browse — as a noun, woody plants, bark, and stems; as a verb, to ingest woody plants, bark, and stems.

Cohort — partner in an activity.

Colt — young male equid.

Comfort behavior — in animal behavior, a term used to include a subset of maintenance behaviors including grooming, scratching, yawning, stretching, wading, and sun-basking.

Comfort behaviors can be solitary or mutual, as with mutual grooming, or mutual fly swatting in horses.

Conspecific — member of the same species.

Cooperative behavior — in animal behavior, the working together of two or more individuals of the same species in an activity that benefits both. A striking example of cooperative behavior in horses can be observed when an entire herd of horses is threatened by an intruder or potential predator. Harem stallions that generally do not co-mingle or tolerate close contact other than the *ritualized posturing* and *elimination marking sequences* will join together and clearly cooperate in defending mares and foals and expelling the intruder. In such a situation the harem mares cooperate in protecting the juveniles by huddling in a circle surrounding the foals. Cooperative behavior among animals of different species is known as *symbiosis*.

Coprophagy — ingestion of feces.

Courtship — in animal behavior, this term is used for the behavior of male and female leading up to mate selection and copulation. In some species, courtship involves elaborate interactive sequences, believed to serve to attract mates, and mates ensure intraspecies partners. So in the whole scheme of animal behavior, the courtship behavior of the horse and other harem breeding equids is relatively simple. For the territorial breeding equids, such as the asses and territorial zebra, the courtship behavior can be seen as slightly more elaborate.

Curiosity — in animal behavior, a tendency to explore novel and non-threatening novel objects and situations. In many species behavior and facial expressions indicating apparent interest in the novelty are common in both adults and young. A good example in horses is the tendency to approach, investigate, and manipulate any non-threatening novel stimuli in their environment. Play in young horses and expressions of curiosity appear to be stimulated by novel situations and objects.

Dam — female parent; mother.

Development — in behavior, the emergence of various forms and complexity of behavior. A synonymous term used in animal behavior is **ontogeny**, or the systematic study of behavioral development. (see Ontogeny)

Dispersion — the density and spacing of a species within its habitat, which is affected by many factors, such as the social composition of the particular group, competition and predation in the habitat, the local terrain (including natural barriers), and the amount and location of available resources.

Displacement activity — a behavior element or sequence that appears out of context and is beleived to be the result of motivational conflict (not sure what to do) or frustration (thwarted from a goal). Common examples that occur in many species are courtship or fighting sequences interrupted momentarily by elements of autogrooming behavior or feeding behavior.

Domestication — the process of humans keeping and usually taming and selectively breeding a species for particular traits, including performance, productivity, fertility, ease of handling, and adaptability to domestic environments. Current evidence indicates that the process of domestication of horses was begun about 8,000 years ago in Eurasia and that the practice of domestication (rather than the movement of already domesticated stock) spread out around the world from there. (For review, see McDonnell 2002)

Dominance — high status in a social system; usually conveys leadership or priority of access to limited resources.

Dominance hierarchy — organized rank of social status. Among species and groups within species there are simple to complex hierarchies, from simple linear relationships across most situations to complicated and/or situation-dependent relationships.

Elimination — expulsion of body wastes; includes defecation, urination, and regurgitation.

Equid — any member of the *Equus* (or horse) family, including domestic horses, Przewalski horses, donkeys, asses, and zebra.

Estrus — sexual attractivity and receptivity in the female; in domestic animals commonly called *heat.*

Ethology — the study of animal behavior with a focus on describing and understanding natural behavior of all species. (see Applied animal behavior)

Feral — animals or populations that were domestic but have been turned out to roam freely. Semi-feral refers to enclosed or managed feral populations.

Filly — young female horse or pony.

Flehmen — a posture in which the head and nose are elevated and sometimes moved side to side while the animal draws air through the mouth and nose. The behavior is believed to serve to carry scents and pheromones into the secondary olfactory (smell) system. In horses, there are many everyday names for this behavior, for example a "lip curl" or "horse laugh."

Foraging behavior — the seeking, apprehending (in the case of carnivores), and consuming of food. In horses, this includes movement to areas with nutritional grasses or browse, as well as the specific behavior and patterns of grazing and browsing and the specific manner of ingesting grasses, roots, fruits, and browse.

Gelding — castrated male horse.

Harem — a breeding system or group consisting of multiple females to one male.

Home range — The area in which an animal or group of animals live. Any part or all of a home range that is guarded is termed a **territory.** So for horses, it is appropriate to refer to the area in which they live as their home range, while for the territorial equids, the males may have a **territory** within the home range. (see Territory)

Hyperphagia — overeating.

Imprinting — A type of automatic experienced-based learning which takes place usually early in an animal's life, during a sensitive or critical period for fixed responses to a particular stimulus. Classic examples are following and attachment responses of neonates to moving beings soon after birth. In horses, the term imprinting in recent decades has been misapplied in an attempt to commercialize the concept of early intensive handling of foals (sold as "Imprint Training," a name which itself represents a contradiction in terms to the behavioral scientist).

Intermale — among males.

Intraspecies — within a species.

Intromission — vaginal penetration of the male copulatory organ.

Jack — mature male donkey.

Jenney or jennes or jennet (all pronounced jen-ee) — mature female donkey.

Lignophagia — ingestion of wood.

Locomotion — in behavior terminology, voluntary movements of the entire body from one place to another on land, water, or through air. Locomotion in horses includes land and water movement.

Maintenance behavior — in the classification of animal and human behavior, the basic survival activities, such as locomotion or exercise, feeding, resting, grooming, shelter, and comfort seeking.

Mare — mature female horse or zebra.

Marking behavior — deposition of urine, feces, or materials from specialized glands. The behavior is presumed to serve to communicate among animals, for example, concerning territory.

Maternal behavior — care of the offspring by the dam.

Mutual grooming — two or more individuals simultaneously grooming one another. (see Allogrooming)

Natal band — An individual horse's family band of birth.

Ontogeny — the animal behavior term that is synonymous with **development**, so the emergence, elaboration, and perfection of behavior. (see Development)

Parturition — the process of birth. In horses, called *foaling*.

Parenting behavior — care of the young by the sire or dam, other related or unrelated conspecifics, or very rarely, even other species. Under natural social conditions the parenting is shared primarily by the dam and harem stallion sire but with some assistance at times from other adult mares, an assistant harem stallion if there is one, and older juveniles and young adults in the harem band.

Paternal behavior — care of offspring by the sire.

Pica — ingesting soil or dirt.

Polydypsia — frequent or copious drinking.

Precocious — born well-developed and able to move about independently.

Przewalski horse — the primitive ancestor of the domestic horse. Once extinct in the wild, some Przewalski horses have recently been reintroduced from zoos and parks to the open range in Mongolia near where they were last known to exist in the wild.

Recumbency — lying down. *Sternal recumbency* refers to lying on the chest. *Lateral recumbency* refers to lying on the side, with legs outstretched.

Ritualized sequences — behavior that occurs in rigidly fixed sequences; an example of somewhat ritualized behavior in horses are the *posturing* and *elimination marking sequences*. (see Section III, Intermale Interactions)

Sentinel — in herds or flocks of prey species, an individual that maintains vigilance and readiness to warn the herd or flock while others are resting or occupied foraging or drinking.

Shaping (behavior) — training (behavior modification) that involves the selective reinforcement of responses that approximate the target behavior. Increasingly stringent response criteria are required for reinforcement until the successful achievement of the target behavior.

Social facilitation — stimulation of a behavior in others by performance of the behavior in one or more individuals.

Social organization — the basic social structure of a species. Horses organize into large herds consisting of harem (family) breeding groups and all-male bachelor bands. (see Band)

Stallion — mature male horse or zebra.

Stereotypy — repeated, often highly stylized, and apparently aimless behavior. Examples of stereotypies in horses are cribbing, and certain forms of head shaking, pawing, weaving, pacing, and stomping.

Stud pile — accumulation of feces from stallions that sequentially mark one another's feces.

Submission — acceptance of low status in a social group; usually includes low priority of access to limited resources.

Subordinant — having relatively low social status in a group.

Territory — an area of the **home range** (see Home range) that is guarded and defended. Among species and populations, depending upon factors such as food availability and reproductive behavior patterns, territories can be more or less permanent or seasonal. Horses under natural conditions are not territorial in the scientific sense of the term. Horses guard and protect their band, but share space with other bands. Among the equids, asses and some zebra stallions are territorial breeders in the sense that they do guard breeding territories, through which females wander. The term *territorial* is commonly misapplied in lay usage to describe a horse's guarding of an unnaturally concentrated resource, such as a water tub, a concentrated palatable feed, or a mare in estrus. The animal behavior or ethology term for guarding behavior (for example, bullying behavior of a horse at a feed bunk or gate to the barn) would be *resource guarding* or *protection*, or *hoarding*, or *food-related aggression*. In horses, food-related aggression or protectiveness is rarely seen outside of domestic husbandry conditions. Horses finding food on their own in open terrain rarely compete aggressively for food or water. Rather than fight over forage or water, they disperse or use sparser patches or follow an established orderly hierarchy at limited watering sites. Most resource-related aggression seen in domestic animals is an artifact of facility designs that fail to accommodate natural spacing and foraging needs of horses.

Trichophagia — ingestion of hair.

Vaulting — jumping onto the back of a moving horse; an equine sport involving individual and team gymnastics performed on the backs of moving horses.

Vocalization — production of sound by means of a vocal apparatus of vertebrates.

Weanling — a foal that has stopped suckling and is not yet one year of age (yearling); in natural social conditions, most foals are still suckling until they are a year or more of age and so the term is mostly limited to domestic foals that are separated from their dams, usually at three to six months of age.

Wild — when compared to feral, or domestic, *wild* refers to animals that are living freely and whose ancestors were never tamed or domesticated. *Captive wild* refers to animals that were born in the wild and then caught for display or breeding in zoos, for example, without taming or domestication, such as *zoo-confined* zebra.

Wink — regarding horse behavior, opening and closing of the vulva (vaginal lips) of the mare during estrus.

Yearling — a young horse born in the previous year, so nearly one to as much as two years old.

Zoo-confined — kept in a zoo.

REFERENCES

Bannikov AG 1971. The Asiatic Wild Ass: neglected relative of the horse. *Animalia* 13: 580–585.

Becker CD, Ginsberg JR 1990. Mother-infant behaviour of wild Grevy's zebra: adaptations for survival in semi-desert East Africa. *Animal Behavior* 40: 1111–1118.

Bekoff M, Byers JA 1998. *Animal Play: Evolutionary, Comparative, and Ecological Perspectives.* Cambridge University Press, Cambridge, UK.

Berger J 1977. Organizational systems and dominance in feral horses in the Grand Canyon. *Behavioral Ecology and Sociobiology* 2: 131–146.

Berger J 1986. *Wild Horses of the Great Basin; Social Competition and Population Size.* The University of Chicago Press, Chicago.

Blakeslee JK 1974. Mother-young relationships and related behavior among free-ranging Appaloosa horses. Master's thesis, Idaho State University, Pocatello, Idaho.

Boy V, Duncan P 1979. Time budgets of Camargue horses I. Developmental changes in the time budgets of foals. *Behaviour* 71: 187–202.

Boyd LE 1980. The natality, foal survivorship, and mare-foal behavior of feral horses in Wyoming's Red Desert. Master's thesis, University of Wyoming, Laramie, Wyoming.

Boyd LE 1986. Behavior problems of equids in zoos. In SL Crowell-Davis, KA Houpt (Eds), *The Veterinary Clinics of North America, Equine Behavior.* WB Saunders Company, Philadelphia, pp 653–654.

Boyd LE 1988. Ontogeny of behavior in Przewalski horses. *Applied Animal Behaviour Science* 21: 41–69.

Boyd LE 1991. The behavior of Przewalski's horses and its importance to their management. *Applied Animal Behaviour Science* 29: 301–318.

Boyd LE, Carbonaro DA, Houpt KA 1988. The 24-hour time budget of Przewalski horses. *Applied Animal Behaviour Science* 21: 5–17.

Boyd LE, Houpt KA 1994. Activity patterns. In LE Boyd, KA Houpt (Eds), *Przewalski's Horse: The History and Biology of an Endangered Species*. State University of New York Press, Albany, New York, pp 195–227.

Boyd L, Kasman L 1986. The marking behavior of the male Przewalski's horses. In D Duvall, D Muller-Schwarze, RM Silverstein (Eds), *Chemical Signals in Vertebrates 4*. Plenum Press, New York, pp 623–626.

Chavatte P 1991. Maternal behaviour in the horse; theory and practical applications to foal rejection and fostering. *Equine Veterinary Education* 3: 215–220.

Crowell-Davis SL 1983. The behavior of Welsh Pony foals and mares. Ph.D. thesis, Cornell University, Ithaca, New York.

Crowell-Davis SL 1986. Developmental behavior. In SL Crowell-Davis, KA Houpt (Eds), *The Veterinary Clinics of North America, Equine Behavior*. WB Saunders Company, Philadelphia, pp 573–590.

Crowell-Davis SL 1986. Mares and foals: normal aggression. *Equine Practice* 8 (7): 30–31.

Crowell-Davis SL 1986. Mares and foals: following, hiding and the recumbency response. *Equine Practice* 8 (8): 34–36.

Crowell-Davis SL 1994. Daytime rest behavior of the Welsh pony (*Equus caballus*) mare and foal. *Applied Animal Behaviour Science* 40: 197–210.

Crowell-Davis SL, Caudle AB 1989. Coprophagy by foals: recognition of maternal feces. *Applied Animal Behaviour Science* 24: 267–272.

Crowell-Davis SL, Houpt KA 1985. Coprophagy by foals: effect of age and possible functions. *Equine Veterinary Journal* 17 (1): 17–19.

Crowell-Davis SL, Houpt KA, Burnham JS 1985. Snapping by foals of *Equus caballus*. *Zeitschrift fur Tierpsychologie* 69: 42–54.

Crowell-Davis SL, Houpt KA, Carnevale J 1985. Feeding and drinking behavior of mares and foals with free access to pasture and water. *Journal of Animal Science* 60: 883–889.

Crowell-Davis SL, Houpt KA, Kane L 1987. Play development in Welsh Pony (*Equus caballus*) foals. *Applied Animal Behaviour Science* 18: 119–131.

Dallaire A 1986. Rest behavior. In SL Crowell-Davis, KA Houpt (Eds), *The Veterinary Clinics of North America, Equine Behavior*. WB Saunders Company, Philadelphia, pp 591–607.

Duncan P 1985. Time budgets of Camargue horses III. Environmental influences. *Behaviour* 92 (1-2): 188–208.

Duncan P, Cowtan P 1980. An unusual choice of habitat helps Camargue horses to avoid blood-sucking horse-flies. *Biology of Behaviour* 5: 55–60.

Evans JW 1989. *Horses: A Guide to Selection, Care, and Enjoyment* (2nd ed.). WH Freeman and Company, New York.

Ewer RF 1968. *The Ethology of Mammals*. Plenum Press, New York.

Fagen RM 1981. *Animal Play Behavior*. Oxford University Press, New York.

Fagen RM, George TK 1977. Play behavior and exercise in young ponies (*Equus caballus L*). *Behavioral Ecology and Sociobiology* 2: 267–269.

Feh C 1988. Social behaviour and relationships of Przewalski horses in Dutch semi-reserves. *Applied Animal Behaviour Science* 21: 71–87.

Feh C 1999. Alliances and reproductive success in Camargue stallions. *Animal Behaviour* 57: 705–713.

Feh C, de Mazières J 1993. Grooming at preferred site reduces heart rate in horses. *Animal Behaviour* 46: 1191–1194.

Feist JD 1971. Behavior of feral horses in the Pryor Mountain Wild Horse Range. Master's thesis, University of Michigan, Ann Arbor, Michigan.

Feist JD, McCullough 1976. Behavior patterns and communication in feral horses. *Zeitschrift fur Tierpsychologie* 41: 337–371.

Francis-Smith K, Wood-Gush DGM 1977. Coprophagy as seen in Thoroughbred foals. *Equine Veterinary Journal* 9: 155–157.

Fraser AF 1992. *The Behaviour of the Horse.* CAB International, Wallingford, UK.

Gardner CD 1983. Grevy's zebra of Samburu Kenya: mothers and foals project in wildlife ecology. Master's thesis, Yale University, New Haven, Connecticut.

Hafez ESE, Williams M, Wierzbowski S 1962. The behaviour of horses. In ESE Hafez (Ed), *The Behaviour of Domestic Animals.* Williams and Wilkins, Baltimore, pp 370–396.

Henry M, McDonnell S, Lodi LD 1991. Pasture breeding behaviour of donkeys under natural and synchronized estrus conditions. *Journal of Reproduction and Fertility Supplement* 44: 77–86.

Hoffmann R 1985. On the development of the social behaviour in immature males of a feral horse population (*Equus przewalskii* f. caballus). *Zeitschrift Saugetierkunde* 50: 302–314.

Hogan ES, Houpt KA, Sweeney K 1988. The effects of enclosure size on social interactions and daily activity patterns of the captive Asiatic wild horse *Equus Przewalski. Applied Animal Behaviour Science* 21: 147–168.

Houpt KA 1984. Foal rejection and other behavioral problems in the postpartum period. *The Compendium on Continuing Education* 6 (3): 144–148.

Houpt KA 1994. Veterinary care. In LE Boyd, KA Houpt (Eds), *Przewalski's Horse*. State University of New York Press, Albany, New York, pp 143–171.

Houpt KA, Boyd L 1994. Social behavior. In LE Boyd, KA Houpt (Eds), *Przewalski's Horse*. State University of New York Press, Albany, New York, pp 229–254.

Houpt KA, McDonnell SM 1993. Equine stereotypies. *The Compendium* 15: 1265–1272.

Houpt KA, Olm D 1984. Foal rejection—A review of 23 cases. *Equine Practice* 6 (7): 38–40.

Houpt KA, Wolski TR 1982. *Domestic Animal Behavior for Veterinarians and Animal Scientists*. Iowa State University Press, Ames, Iowa.

Joubert E 1972. The social organization and associated behaviour in the Hartmann zebra (*Equus zebra hartmannae*). *Madoqua Seriale I* (6): 17–56.

Keiper RR 1985. *The Assateague Ponies*. Tidewater Publishers, Centreville, Maryland.

Keiper RR 1988. Social interactions of the Przewalski horse (*Equus przewalskii* Poliakov, 1881) herd at the Munich Zoo. *Applied Animal Behaviour Science* 21: 89–97.

Keiper RR, Berger J 1982. Refuge-seeking and pest avoidance by feral horses in desert and island environments. *Applied Animal Ethology* 9: 111–120.

Keiper RR, Keenan MA 1980. Nocturnal activity patterns of feral ponies. *Journal of Mammalogy* 61: 116–118.

Klimov A 1988. Spatial-ethological investigation of the herd of

Przewalski horses in Askania-Nova. *Applied Animal Behaviour Science* 21: 99–115.

Klingel H 1967. Soziale organization und verhalten freilebender Steppenzebras (*Equus quagga*). *Zeitschrift fur Tierpsychologie* 24: 580–624.

Klingel H 1969. Reproduction in Plains zebra *Equus burchelli boehmi Mitchie*: behaviour and ecological factors. *Journal of Reproduction and Fertility Supplement* 6: 339–345.

Klingel H 1975. Social organization of reproduction in equids. *Journal of Reproduction and Fertility Supplement* 23: 7–11.

Klingel H 1998. Observations on social organization and behaviour of African and Asiatic wild asses (*Equus africanus* and *Equus hemionus*). *Applied Animal Behaviour Science* 60: 103–113.

Mayes E, Duncan P 1986. Temporal patterns of feeding in free-ranging horses. *Behaviour* 96: 105–129.

McBane S 1987. *Behaviour Problems in Horses*. David and Charles, North Pomfret, Vermont.

McCort WD 1980. The behavior and social organization of feral asses (*Equus asinus*) on Ossabaw Island, Georgia. Ph.D. thesis, Pennsylvania State University, State College, Pennsylvania.

McCort WD 1984. Behavior of feral horses and ponies. *Journal of Animal Science* 58 (2): 493–499.

McDonnell SM 1986. Reproductive behavior of the stallion. In KA Houpt, SL Crowell-Davis (Eds), *Veterinary Clinics of North America Equine Practice* 2 (3)(Behavior): 535–555.

McDonnell SM 1992. Normal and abnormal sexual behavior. In TL Blanchard, DD Varner (Eds), *Veterinary Clinics of North America Equine Practice* 8 (1) (Stallion Management): 71–89.

McDonnell SM 2002. Behaviour of horses. In P Jensen (Ed), *The Ethology of Domestic Animals*, CABI Publishing, New York, pp 119–129.

McDonnell SM, Haviland JCS 1995. Agnostic ethogram of the equid bachelor band. *Applied Animal Behaviour Science* 43: 147–188.

McDonnell SM, Henry M, Bristol F 1991. Spontaneous erection and masturbation in equids. *Journal of Reproduction and Fertility Supplement* 44: 664–665.

McDonnell SM, Poulin A 2002. Equid play ethogram. *Applied Animal Behaviour Science* 78: 263-290.

McFarland D 1987. *The Oxford Companion to Animal Behaviour*. Oxford University Press, New York.

McGreevy PD 1996. *Why does my horse...?* Trafalgar Square, London.

McGreevy PD, Hawson LA, Habermann TC, Cattle SR 2001. Geophagia in horses: a short note on 13 cases. *Applied Animal Behaviour Science* 71: 119–215.

Miller RW 1981. Male aggression, dominance, and breeding behavior in Red Desert feral horses. *Zeitschrift fur Tierpsychologie* 57: 340–351.

Miller RW 1974. *Western Horse Behavior and Training*. Doubleday, New York.

Moehlman PD 1974. Behavior and ecology of feral asses (*Equus asinus*). Ph.D. dissertation. University of Wisconsin, Madison, Wisconsin.

Moehlman PD 1998. Behavioral patterns and communication in feral asses (*Equus africanus*). *Applied Animal Behaviour Science* 60: 125–169.

Odberg FO 1973. An interpretation of pawing in the horse. *Saugetier Klundliche-Mitteilungen* 21: 1–12.

Pellegrini SW 1971. Home range, territoriality and movement patterns of horses in the Wassuk Range of western Nevada. Master's thesis, University of Nevada, Reno, Nevada.

Penzhorn BL 1984. A long-term study of social organization and behaviour of Cape Mountain Zebras *Equus zebra zebra*. *Zeitschrift fur Tierpsychologie* 64: 97–146.

Prince D 1987. Stable vices. In S McBane, *Behaviour Problems in Horses*. David and Charles, North Pomfret, Vermont, pp 115–122.

Richardson C 1998. *The Horse Breakers*. JA Allen, London.

Rifa H 1990. Social facilitation in the horse (*Equus caballus*). *Applied Animal Behaviour Science* 25: 167–176.

Rudman R, Keiper RR 1991. The body condition of feral ponies on Assateague Island. *Equine Veterinary Journal* 23 (6): 453–456.

Salter RE, Hudson RJ 1979. Feeding ecology of feral horses in Western Alberta. *Journal of Range Management* 32: 221–225.

Salter RE, Hudson RJ 1982. Social organization of feral horses in western Canada. *Applied Animal Behaviour Science* 8: 207–223.

Schilder MBH 1988. Dominance relationships between adult plains zebra stallions in semi-captivity. *Behaviour* 104: 300–319.

Schilder MBH 1990. Intervention in a herd of semi-captive plains zebra. *Behaviour* 112: 53-83.

Schilder MBH, Boer PL 1987. Ethological investigations on a herd of Plains Zebra in a safari park: Time budgets, reproduction and food competition. *Applied Animal Behaviour Science* 18: 45–56.

Schilder MBH, van Hoof JA, van Geer-Plesman CJ, Wensing JB 1984. A quantitative analysis of facial expression in the Plains Zebra. *Zeitschrift fur Tierpsychologie* 66: 11–32.

Schneider KM 1930. Das flehmen. *Zoologischer Garten* 3: 183–198.

Schoen AMS, Banks EM, Curtis SE 1976. Behavior of young Shetland and Welsh Ponies (*Equus caballus*). *Biology of Behavior* 1: 192–216.

Stahlbaum CC, Houpt KA 1989. The role of flehmen response in the behavioural repertoire of the stallion. *Physiology and Behavior* 45: 1207–1214.

Stevens EF 1987. Ecological and demographic influences of social behavior, harem stability, and male reproductive success in feral horses (*Equus caballus*). Ph.D. dissertation, University of North Carolina, Chapel Hill, North Carolina.

Syme GJ, Syme LA 1979. *Social Structure in Farm Animals*. Elsevier, New York.

Tembrock G 1968. Land mammals. In TA Sebeok (Ed), *Animal Communication: Techniques of Study and Results of Research*. Indiana University Press, Bloomington, Indiana, pp 338–404.

Tilson RL, Sweeny KA, Binczik GA, Reindl NJ 1988. Buddies and bullies: social structure of a bachelor group of Przewalski horses. *Applied Animal Behaviour Science* 21: 169–185.

Turner JW, Perkins A, Kirkpatrick JF 1981. Elimination marking behavior in feral horses. *Canadian Journal of Zoology* 59: 1561–1566.

Tyler SJ 1972. Behavior and social organization of the semi-feral ponies. *Animal Behaviour Monograph* 5.

Waring GH 1983. *Horse Behavior: The Behavioral Traits and Applications of Domestic and Wild Horses, Including Ponies*. Noyes Publications, Park Ridge, New Jersey.

Waring GH 2002. *Horse Behavior: The Behavioral Traits and Applications of Domestic and Wild Horses, Including Ponies.* (2nd ed.) Noyes Publications, Park Ridge, New Jersey.

Wells SM, von Goldschmidt-Rothschild B 1979. Social behaviour and relationships in a herd of Camargue horses. *Zeitschrift fur Tierpsychologie* 49: 363–380.

Welsh DA 1975. Population, behavioural, and grazing ecology of the horses of Sable Island, Nova Scotia. Ph.D. thesis, Dalhousie University, Halifax, Canada.

Wolski TR, Houpt KA, Aronson R 1980. The role of the senses in mare-foal recognition. *Applied Animal Ethology* 6: 121–138.

Zeeb K 1959. Die 'unterlegenheitsgebarde' des noch nicht ausgewachsenen. Pierdes (*Equus caballus*). *Zeitschrift fur Tierpsychologie* 16: 489–496.

INDEX

*Italicized words represent behavior entries

ABOUT the AUTHOR

SUE MILLER MCDONNELL is a native Pennsylvanian, raised in a dairy farming family in the anthracite coal regions north of Scranton. She holds a 1982 master's degree in psychology from West Chester University and a 1985 Ph.D. in reproductive physiology and behavior from the University of Delaware. She completed post-doctoral study in clinical veterinary reproduction with Dr. Bob Kenney at the University of Pennsylvania's New Bolton Center in 1987 and became board certified in applied animal behavior in 1991.

She is the founder of the Equine Behavior Program at the University of Pennsylvania School of Veterinary Medicine, where her work includes clinical, research, and teaching activities focused on horse behavior. Dr. McDonnell is known internationally for her research-based scientific approach to equine behavior. She has conducted studies for The National Institutes of Health on the physiology and pharmacology of erection and ejaculation in horses and men. She also has studied equids throughout the world.

Dr. McDonnell maintains a semi-feral herd of ponies for the study of their physiology and behavior under semi-natural conditions. This affords veterinary and animal behavior students the opportunity for long-term observation of equine social and developmental behavior and for first-hand comparison of horse behavior under free-running and traditional domestic conditions.

Dr. McDonnell is particularly well known for her expertise with stallion sexual behavior dysfunction. She consults with horse owners, managers, and veterinarians throughout the United States and the world on breeding behavior problems.

Notes

Notes

Notes

Notes

Notes

Notes

Notes

Notes

Notes

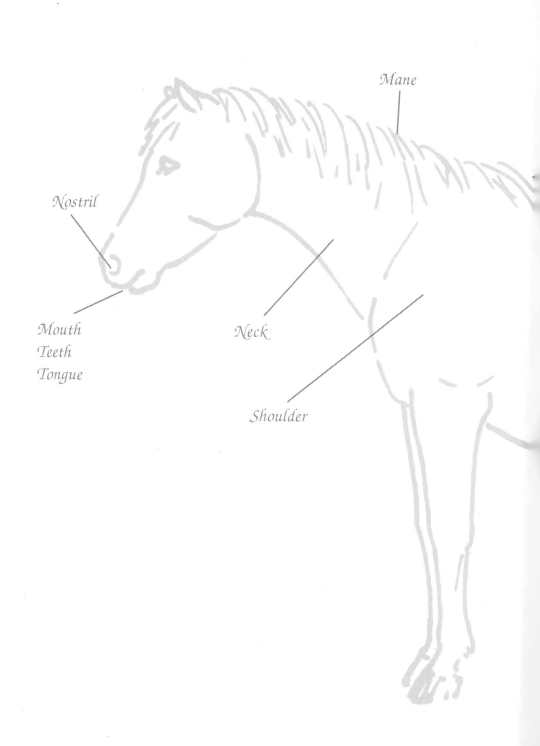

Mane

Nostril

Mouth
Teeth
Tongue

Neck

Shoulder